THE OPEN UNIVERSITY

Arts : A Third Level Course
Twentieth Century Poetry

Units 2-3

THOMAS HARDY

Prepared by Cicely Havely for the Course Team

21.6.79.

The Open University Press

Cover   Photograph of Thomas Hardy from the Mansell Collection

The Open University Press
Walton Hall   Milton Keynes
MK7 6AA

First published 1975. Reprinted 1977(with corrections)

Designed by the Media Development Group of The Open University.

Printed in Great Britain by
EYRE AND SPOTTISWOODE LIMITED
AT GROSVENOR PRESS PORTSMOUTH

ISBN 0 335 05101 4

This text forms part of an Open University course. The complete list of units in the course appears at the end of this text.

For general availability of supporting material referred to in this text please write to: Open University Educational Enterprises Limited, 12 Cofferidge Close, Stony Stratford, Milton Keynes, MK11 1BY, Great Britain.

Further information on Open University courses may be obtained from the Admissions Office, The Open University, P.O. Box 48, Walton Hall, Milton Keynes, MK7 6AB.

1.2

CONTENTS   UNITS 2–3

PART 1

PART 2

I would like to thank my colleagues Alasdair Clayre, Nick Furbank, Arnold Kettle, Roger Lewis, Graham Martin, Nuala O'Faolain, and John Purkis for their advice.

I should also like to thank my friend Marjorie Crampton Smith for further encouragement and for hours of invigorating conversation about poetry: and Alison Andrews for her unfailing skill and patience in dealing with a chaotic manuscript.

1   INTRODUCTION

1.1   Thomas Hardy was born in 1840 and died in 1928. A long life by any standards and in any period, but perhaps its real length is properly measured by the **vast** differences between the kind of world in which he lived, and the world in which he died. He was born before Tennyson had achieved full recognition, and he died more than a decade after T. S. Eliot's 'Love Song of J. Alfred Prufrock' was published. The major poets writing at the time of his death tended, naturally enough, to call him a Victorian; in age he was not of their generation. Now, and for reasons that I hope will be made clear, it seems less appropriate to think of him as a chance survivor of the nineteenth century. But the simplest and best reason for including him in this course must be that he wrote about three-quarters of his poetry within the period we are studying. Indeed, some of his finest work of all was written in the strangely crucial year 1912: when you read the final section of Part 1 of these units, ask yourself whether this was only coincidental.

1.2   His novels were all written before the nineteenth century closed, and so for thirty years Hardy was able to devote himself to being a poet. Poetry was his first love, and he had rather a poor opinion of novels in general, including his own. Some critics have tended to regard the poems as the scraps left over from making the novels, and most who have considered both poetry and prose have seen the former as in some way dependent on, and conditioned by, the novels. But such attitudes degrade the poetry, which has an independent status. Novelist and poet in Hardy can be separated; and indeed I think they need to be separated, especially for the sake of the poems, which have been overshadowed too long. I have occasionally referred to Hardy's work as a novelist, but each time I was aware that I could have avoided the reference. The points I make would I hope have been just even if Hardy had never written a single novel. Such as they are, the references are very general, and I have used them because I believed they helped me say what I wanted more quickly. You will not need any knowledge of Hardy's novels before you read his poetry.

1.3   The set text for these units is *Poems of Thomas Hardy, A New Selection*: selected, with an introduction and notes, by T. R. Creighton, Macmillan, 1974. It is a large selection, though it consists of only about one quarter of Hardy's published poems. And we shall be looking at considerably less than one quarter of Creighton's selection. Obviously you would do well to read as many more of the poems as you can. I have tried to follow Creighton's lead and recommend something like a miniaturized cross-section of Hardy's poetry. But it is as well to realize from the beginning that no two readers ever seem likely to agree about what such a cross-section should include.

1.4   Make full use of Creighton's introduction and notes. I do not always agree with his interpretations, but that is unimportant. I do not always agree with the other critics I have quoted in these units, nor with those whose work on Hardy has been included in the Course Reader.[1]

1.5   I have not tried to put before you a potted, though respectable version of the best critical opinion about Hardy's poetry. This is partly for the good reason that we want to leave you free to make up your own mind, and partly for the not so good reason that no such coherent body exists. Part 1, Sections 2–6 will discuss groups of thematically linked poems. The approach is tentative and exploratory, rather than tendentious. Part 2, on the other hand, is more tendentious and argumentative. You will be better equipped to fight back if you have already studied some of Hardy's poetry, even though it can only be a small proportion of his total achievement.

[1]Graham Martin and P. N. Furbank (eds.) (1975) *Twentieth Century Poetry: Critical Essays and Documents*, The Open University Press.

2 NARRATIVE POEMS

2.1 Despite what I said in the Introduction about the relevance of the novels, it seems appropriate (when looking for a place to begin) to choose poems that tell a story, for the convenient reason that Hardy was an established novelist long before he published any poetry. Indeed, in all his poetry, the instinct to tell a story remains strong. Read as much as you wish of Part V of your anthology, though we shall only discuss 'The Bride-Night Fire', 'Valenciennes', 'San Sebastian' and 'A Tramp Woman's Tragedy'. Make *brief* notes on such things as style, content, tone, what each poem is about – or indeed about anything that strikes you as being particularly good (or bad) or interesting. What does Hardy want to achieve in each poem, and how does he set about it? Put down what you feel is important not after a single cursory reading, but after concentrated, attentive reading. Number the stanzas for reference.

2.2 After such vague questions, you might have written almost anything. I hope you wanted to write down your response, and did not feel that it was a dreary chore to be undertaken so that you might feel the benefit of it some day.

I wonder if any part of your notes looked like this:

> *The Bride-Night Fire:* 19 stanzas, the first of 7 lines, last of 8. The remainder a random arrangement of 5 and 6 line stanzas. *Rhythm:* a basic anapaestic (short-short-long) pattern with frequent variations and inversions. *Rhyme:* a b, followed by 2, 3 or 4 a's and the last line b. The last stanza starts with 2 a's, but otherwise the same.

Suppose your notes are a bit like that: did you make them because you wanted to, or because it was the only thing you could think of, or because you felt you ought to? Notes like that are fine as far as they go, but they do not go far enough. They do not begin to suggest the flavour of the poems or what kind of effect is achieved by the technical means you have so painstakingly recorded. The effect of rhythm and rhyme you will be aware of (though you may not be able to define it) the first time you read the poem and every time afterwards. But when you write down a b a a a b you are not reading at all, but counting.

2.3 Take it another way. Suppose when you read 'The Bride-Night Fire' you said: 'Rollicking – that's the only word for it'. (It is not of course: what is any poem likely to be worth that can be summed up in a single word?) Then the next step is to find out how (so to speak) it rollicks. The story moves at great pace, not stopping for a moment's sympathy for Naibour Sweatley, reduced to cinders on his wedding night. But it is not unduly callous. Nor is the speed merely incidental: it is also *effective*. It is inseparable from the feeling of vigour and vitality which the poem communicates. The pace is partly achieved through the headlong anapaestic rhythms and thus a mechanical means reinforces or contributes to what is not mechanical at all. You do not even need to know the word anapaestic to be able to recognize this and analyse it. Notice how the pace of the rhythm literally quickens the erotic interest of the poem. Would it be as lusty in slow iambics? As it is, the rhythm is perfectly appropriate for lovers who meet 'at junketings, maypoles and flings'.

It may be that you did not make any kind of note referring to the speed of this poem. But that would surely not be because you did not feel its speed; rather, you were not aware that you had noticed it. If there are handy hints for what is generally but rather inanely known as 'practical criticism' then among the first must be 'Learn to be conscious of your response.'

2.4 What else, if anything, makes 'The Bride-Night Fire', 'rollicking'? Rhyme, like rhythm can be mechanically analysed, and it is easy enough to identify the scheme here. But how does it work?

With only two different rhymes in each stanza in spite of the varying number of lines, the effect is compact and firm. The uncertainty as you begin each stanza as to how many 'a' rhymes there will be works together with the onward plunge of the rhythm. The final 'b' rhyme ties up each stanza and has a kind of braking effect. And each successive 'a b' opening makes a momentary slowing down before the fast and furious pace is picked up again. The random and headlong movement is controlled – but only just.

2.5 ■ 'The Bride-Night Fire' is not a very serious poem, but it has been seriously and carefully made. Everything in it has been directed to one end and all its elements work together. Again, the dialect is something you cannot fail to notice, but what exactly does it contribute?

Discussion

A rusticity appropriate to a rustic love story? But that is a rather condescending way of putting it, and condescending is surely what this poem is not. It would be nearer the mark to say that by telling the story of Tim and his sweetheart in a dialect which is approximately that of the lovers themselves the narrator cuts the distance between himself and his subject, and declares his sympathy. But the tone is given a little ironic twist by the fact that if you look carefully at what Barbree says her idiom, in contrast with her accent, is rather high-flown and literary:

> 'I think I mid almost ha'borne it,' she said
>   'Had my griefs one by one come to hand;
> But O, to be slave to thik husbird, for bread,
> And then, upon top o'that, driven to wed,
> And then, upon top o'that, burnt out o'bed,
>   Is more than my nater can stand!'

Look at the contrast between lines 3 and 4, and 5: the first two the stuff of Victorian melodrama, the third pure farce, and no slackening of pace between them. It is worth noticing once again that we do not for one minute think of the fire as a tragedy. This should remind us that the main purpose of this poem seems to be to tell a story in a lively and entertaining manner, and that if we were simply given the bare outline of the narrative we would immediately recognize that there is more than one way of telling it.

2.6 Hardy's way is to leave out everything that does not conform to his single point of view: he is on the side of the lovers. This technique of omitting what is not essential to the storyteller's purpose is a fundamental part of ballad tradition, and as Thom Gunn says in the radio programme *Hardy and the Ballads* it is a technique which Hardy adapts for many different kinds of poetry, and not just for pieces like 'The Bride-Night Fire' which are unmistakably based on traditional ballad forms.[2] Excision, or cutting away of various kinds seems to be the fundamental principle of construction here. Notice how laconic the poem is ('. . . throw over pu'pit the names of the pair') and how ironic: both qualities which make for speed by moving quickly over things unsaid. Indeed, all humour is essentially quick. A joke may be a long time telling (though that is not the case here) but when the punch line comes, the humour is achieved in a flash. And so it is not just rhyme and rhythm which keep the poem moving at such a pace, but also the narrative technique and the tone. ■

[2]See Appendix 1, p 58

2.7 ■ I do not want to spend as long on the other poems I have asked you to read. But if you have not already done so, will you think for a while about why, or for what purpose, they were written.

Discussion

There must be some reason for a poem's existence, and even the answer 'because the poet wanted to write it' implies something important. Other answers might be 'to tell a story' or 'to give pleasure', or 'to make you think a bit'. None of these poems seems to have a very lofty purpose, just as none of them seems to want to communicate anything that is difficult to get hold of. You probably felt you understood these poems perfectly the first time you read them, and I am not going to say that they are full of hidden complexities that a first reading misses. But how are these strong clear effects achieved – seemingly with so little effort?

2.8 There seems no doubt that Hardy did not just want to write a poem: he knew what he wanted to say, and does it unerringly – something not easy to achieve. Look for example at 'Valenciennes'. The first six stanzas do not seem to be going anywhere in particular. At a first reading you may think them simply a stirring, but rather haphazard account of the horrors of a bombardment, recalled by one of the common soldiery. Then the corporal describes the wound to his head, and the surgery, and then comes stanza 11, moving in its understatement:

> I never hear the zummer hums
> O' bees; and don' know when the cuckoo comes;
> But night and day I hear the bombs
> We threw at Valencieën . . .

(Throughout, the name of the town has to be pronounced Vàl-en-seèn.) When you get to this point, the rightness of the stanza is a kind of proof that everything that has gone before has been leading up to this. The din of the battle was emphasized in the first stanza. Notice how the word 'hummed' ('And from our mortars tons of iron hummed') is picked up again in the stanza just quoted. Maybe you think the words are too widely separated for the contrast to be effective. Perhaps also it is only when you reach stanza 11 that the full significance of stanza 4 is revealed:

> 'Twas said that we'd no business there
> A-topperèn the French for disagreën;
> However, that's not my affair –
> We were at Valencieën.

Corp'l Tullidge does not think too much about what he is doing, but he admits that his (and the English army's) right to be there can be questioned. Then, in stanza 11 the same question is repeated, not explicitly (for the narration is kept within the character of the speaker) but implicitly, by the poet's careful insinuation. The corporal is a simple, kindly man ('And harmless townsfolk fell to die' – stanza 6) whose natural business is not with battles, but with the things which his wound has spoiled for him.

2.9 Yet although the poem is moving, it is rigorously unsentimental. The poem could well have ended with stanza 11; instead, Hardy chose to add three more stanzas, which deliberately reduce the emotional pitch. Stanza 12 is an ironic understatement which clears the way for the paradoxes of the last two stanzas. The corporal is 'sort o' glad' he fought at Valencieën: and this simple revelation invests the final stanza with a colossal ambiguity. Have the terrors of the siege even blighted the old soldier's hopes of heaven? Or does he feel rather elated at the prospect of defending the pearly gates? (Next time we assume he will be inside the city.) In fact you cannot choose one interpretation and leave the other: you have to accept the paradox. This is neither a pro- nor anti-war poem. It is a poem about a man who has lost almost everything that makes life worth living, and yet still finds zest in the idea of war.

In 'San Sebastian' and 'A Tramp Woman's Tragedy' there is a similar sympathetic insight into the more inexplicable areas of the human consciousness. In 'San Sebastian' the daughter is in no biological sense the child of the rape her father committed; but she is the offspring of his guilt. In the second poem, a moment's folly leads to terrible consequences, undreamt of by the tramp woman. The woman is not really blamed for her wantonness: the tragedy springs from the terrible disproportion between intention and consequence. Both these poems share an uncomfortable awareness that ordinary human beings are incapable of foreseeing all the possible consequences of their action. But Hardy does not see just the single moment, the single action: he sees the span of time bound together, and for every action, a sequel. He frequently writes about the common, hopeless pain of hindsight: if we had known then what we know now, how differently we would have behaved. Later, we shall see that it was just this sort of regret which characterized some of his finest and most personal poems. These narrative poems are not personal: they are perhaps case studies of a kind. The soldier in the ferment of battle, the tramp woman with no husband or home, are types of those who cannot give thought to the morrow. ◾

2.10   Maybe it was Hardy's experience as a novelist that made him such a keen observer of the oddities of human nature. I prefer to think of him as an avid collector of curiosities, for it was not only the quirks of personality that he treasured; he cherished odd little incidents of all kinds.

A far greater debt which the poems may owe to the novels is their lucidity. These stories are told clearly and without fuss, and almost without exception the rest of Hardy's poetry says what he wants to say in ways that are immediately open to the reader. There is no vagueness or obscurity in his work. He wrote his novels for readers who wanted unambiguous narratives, and consciously or not, his poetry is addressed to the same audience. Such a criterion does not exclude complexity or profundity, but it was the faith of most of the great nineteenth-century novelists that whatever could exist, could be unambiguously communicated. Ezra Pound, who admired Hardy very much, said of his poetry, 'Now *there* is a clarity. There is the harvest of having written 20 novels first.' (Pound: Letters 294.) Such consistent clarity means that Hardy does not present his reader with the besetting obscurities and problems of comprehension which are virtually endemic to 'modernist' poetry. However, it must not be thought that because he is clear, he lacks all mystery. Indeed, to be paradoxical, the heart of his mystery is that clarity does not preclude mystery. Thom Gunn, in the radio programme I have already mentioned, suggests that a useful way of exploring this paradox is to look at Hardy's relationship with the ballads – not Hardy's own ballads, but the traditional, anonymous poetry that has survived through oral tradition. Gunn sees in such poetry the same clarity of essential detail combined with an impersonal, uninvolved narrative technique that characterizes the whole body of Hardy's verse. The four ballads we have looked at are in fact not very like the best of the Border Ballads, such as 'Sir Patrick Spens' or 'Tam Lin', if only because the detailing of the incidents is more specific. 'The Bride-Night Fire' and 'Valenciennes' are much more like the later broadside ballads, or even a certain type of anecdotal Victorian song. But Gunn is right to stress the importance of the ballad style to Hardy, for the ballads exerted a far greater influence on Hardy's work than the poetry of his immediate predecessors or of his contemporaries. His novels show how aware he was of the drastic changes that were taking place in the centuries-old patterns of rural life. If this is not a very prominent theme in the poetry, nevertheless the continual echoes from the ballads are evidence of the value he found in such long-lived survivors from the past.

3 MUSIC, METRE AND STRUCTURE

3.1 Both traditional and broadside ballads should be thought of as the 'lyrics' for songs. Music was the almost inevitable accompaniment to one of the most important influences on Hardy's poetry. But there is more music in Hardy's poetry than this silent presence. Read: 'One We Knew' (p 88), 'A Church Romance'* (p 89), 'The Self-Unseeing'* (p 90), 'The House of Hospitalities' (p 92), 'Afternoon Service at Mellstock' (p 93), 'To My Father's Violin' (p 97), 'Silences' (p 99), 'Lost Love' (p 48), 'A Duettist to her Pianoforte'* (p 47), and 'The Choirmaster's Burial'* (p 225).

Hardy was born into a family where music was very important. His grandfather, father and uncle played bass, tenor and treble viols for their church, and directed the choir. Thomas Hardy (son and grandson of other Thomases) never heard the choir, which was disbanded when he was still a baby, but his father's reminiscences are used in both the novels and the poems.

> Conducting the church choir all the year round involved carol-playing and singing at Christmas, which Thomas Hardy the Second loved as much as did his father. In addition to the ordinary practice, the work of preparing and copying carols a month of evenings beforehand was not light, and incidental expenses were appreciable. The parish being a large and scattered one, it was the custom of Thomas Hardy the First to assemble the rather perfunctory rank-and-file of the choir at his house; and this necessitated suppers, and suppers demanded (in those days) plenty of liquor. This was especially the case on Christmas Eve itself, when the rule was to go to the northern part of the parish and play at every house before supper; then to return to Brockhampton and sit over the meal till twelve o'clock, during which interval a good deal was consumed at the Hardy's expense, the choir being mainly poor men and hungry. They then started for the other parts of the parish, and did not get home till all was finished at about six in the morning, the performers themselves feeling 'no more than malkins'[3] in church next day, as they used to declare. (Florence Emily Hardy *The Life of Thomas Hardy*, p 12.)

Hardy's father

> . . . was good . . . when young, at hornpipes and jigs, and other folk-dances, performing them with all the old movements of leg-crossing and hop, to the delight of the children, till warned by his wife that this fast perishing style might tend to teach them what it was not quite necessary they should be

*Poems marked thus will be studied in detail; but read as many of the others as you can.
[3]*malkin* a damp rag for swabbing out an oven.

familiar with, the more genteel 'country-dance' having superseded the former. (Hardy *Life*, p 13.)

3.2 As the poem 'One We Knew' illustrates, Hardy was fascinated by the personal links with the distant past which the memories of his relatives of an older generation could give him. M. H., Hardy's maternal grandmother, could remember the French Revolution: her grandson was to outlive the year of the General Strike. The sonnet 'A Church Romance' is based on another family memory.

> Mrs Hardy once described him [her husband] to her son as he was when she first set eyes on him in the now removed west gallery of Stinsford Church, appearing to her more travelled glance (she had lived for a time in London, Weymouth and other towns) and somewhat satirical vision, 'rather amusingly old-fashioned, in spite of being decidedly good-looking—wearing the blue swallow-tailed coat with gilt embossed buttons then customary, a red and black flowered waistcoat, Wellington boots,[4] and French-blue trousers'. (Hardy *Life* p 13.)

In his poetic account of his parents' first meeting, the energy the musician puts into his playing arouses and communicates love. Not that love songs are being played: the music is, very emphatically, that of familiar hymns – 'New Sabbath or Mount Ephraim'. But his manner is more important than the tune he plays:

> One strenuous viol's inspirer seemed to throw
> A message from his string to her below,
> Which said: 'I claim thee as my own forthright.'

– and this 'in her prides' despite'. Hardy dramatizes the ironies of the prose account ('her more travelled glance . . . and somewhat satirical vision') and hints in the poem that a more serious division needs to be overcome: 'high pew' suggests the secluded box pew of the big house. Notice in particular how careful Hardy is to make the poem say exactly what he wants to say, even at the cost of a certain earnest awkwardness. The oddness of the phrase 'One strenuous viol's inspirer' demands our attention, and we feel that for Hardy an achieved concentration of meaning outweighs tongue-twisting awkwardness. Indeed, the repeated s-sounds suggest that Hardy deliberately made the phrase difficult to say. It is not a case of sound echoing sense, but of sound being used as a kind of brake. This, after all, is a crucial point in the narrative, and the reader must slow down to take it in.

The story is slight enough. What power the poem has to move us (and it may not be much) resides in the balance between the past and what followed. Structurally the poem makes use of one of the sonnet's traditional pivots: the break between the quatrains and the sestet. Hardy underlines the first/later contrast with very careful syntax:

> Thus their hearts' bond began, in due time signed.
> And long years thence, when Age had scared Romance . . .

3.3 ■ I expect you will have noticed similar contrasts in time in other poems of this group. Hardy frequently compares the past with the present – with himself, that is,

---

[4] *Not* gum boots!

at the time of writing. Sometimes this is simple nostalgia. But in 'A Church Romance' the contrast is not between then and now, but between *first* and *later*. Why do you think Hardy finds the difference worth writing about?

Discussion

To be very gnomic for a moment, Hardy always seemed to find the differences in things worth writing about. Here, we can define the difference more precisely by saying that he compares the moment as it happened, with the moment as *memory*. There is no tragedy in the comparison, for no one has died, nor has the marriage been unhappy. There is only the common poignancy of ageing, and time passed. This part of your anthology is called *The Past and the Present*, and this group of poems, together with the ballad 'San Sebastian' may well already have suggested to you that memory is a theme of great importance in this poetry. Memories are indeed the most important, and often the most troubling of the ghosts that crowd Hardy's imagination. There is nothing particularly troubling in this memory. Hardy says nothing about regret for the past, but perhaps a kind of pain is implied in the phrase 'break upon her mind'. Obviously this little poem contains nothing like the remorse for the consequences of past action which figured in 'San Sebastian' and 'The Tramp Woman's Tragedy', and yet all three poems are related by Hardy's interest in what is expressed in the simple understatement 'the way things turn out'. ∎

The association of music and memory is common enough. Most castaways seem to choose their desert island discs for nostalgic reasons. But music does not bring back the past for Hardy. The woman of 'A Church Romance' does not hear Mount Ephraim, and *then* remember 'him as minstrel, ardent, young and trim'. For her, the music belongs to the past, and so it is with the best of Hardy's poetry that is about music, or in which music plays an important part.

3.4 ∎ Is this only an insignificant quirk of personality? It has often been said that 'the way things turn out' is, in Hardy's work, far more often bad than good; and certainly one of the factors in his poetry that contributes to the impression that times will get worse is the repeated assertion that the past was richer, or more vital, or more loving than the present. He does not say in so many words that the music has gone out of life, but he frequently implies it, and to understand what he means, look again at this group of poems for the values he associates with music.

Discussion

The harmonies of music comment in various ways on the harmoniousness of human relationships. Sometimes the comment is bitterly ironical. In 'Lost Love' (p 48) the tunes are the same, but their power of pleasing has gone. Music is not valued so much for itself, as for its life-enhancing social qualities. And although there is plenty of evidence elsewhere that Hardy claimed to appreciate classical music, in his poetry it is popular music – hymns, dances, songs – that have his special attention. In 'A Duettist to her Pianoforte' (p 47) he mentions some Victorian parlour favourites

> I fain would second her, strike to her stroke,
> As when she was by,
> Aye, even from the ancient clamorous 'Fall
> Of Paris', or 'Battle of Prague' withal,
> To the 'Roving Minstrels', or 'Elfin Call'
> Sung soft as a sigh . . .

perhaps there is a little gentle irony in the word 'clamorous', but there is not a shadow of condescension. A reference to one of these pieces in a letter dated 30 December 1919 makes it clear that Hardy found nothing to smile at in such programme music:

> I am sorry to say that your appeal for a poem that should be worthy of the event of the 8th August 1918 reaches me at too late a time of life to attempt it . . . The outline of such a poem, which you very cleverly sketch, is striking, and ought to result at the hands of somebody or other who may undertake it, in a literary parallel to the 'Battle of Prague' – a piece of music which ceased to be known long before your time, but was extraordinarily popular in its day – reproducing the crashing of guns nearer and nearer, the groans of the wounded, and the final fulfilment, with great fidelity.
> (Hardy *Life* p 395.)

Perhaps he valued such pieces too highly, or perhaps we deride them too much. From the *Life* it is clear that he would read anything that was recommended to him as necessary that a well-educated man should know, without bothering too much about what was good and what was not. Maybe the same was true of his musical tastes. I do not mean to sneer at Hardy, but ballad tunes, country dances and some hymn tunes have all been given the cultural seal of approval, whereas 'The Battle of Prague' and 'Elfin Call' have not – at least, not quite. The music which has associative values for Hardy is not only what we like to think of as the genuinely popular music, sanctified by the affectionate use of many generations. But although the music of the Victorian bourgeoisie was of more artificial manufacture, it too was popular in the sense that it enjoyed wide circulation. Nor can there be any doubt that it was powerfully emotive, and it was for this, surely, that Hardy valued it. He could rely on an audience in the thousands of middle-class drawing rooms where hearts have thrilled to the tremolo passages of ' "Elfin Call" Sung soft as a sigh'. ■

'A Duettist to her Pianoforte' is too clumsy to be successful. A heavy weight of sentiment is invested not in the music, but the very Victorian instrument that produced it, with its 'pleated show of silk, now hoar'. Notice how the elaborate metre suggests just the kind of fussy, virtuoso music the duettists might have played, each stanza ending with a plaintive diminuendo – 'So it's hushed, hushed, hushed, you are for me!' There is a curious tension between the almost too-musical quality of the metre and the prosaic deliberation of the diction. There is something over-anxious about words and phrases like counterchord; upping ghosts; achefully; polyphones, plaints and quavers. He aims not just at a powerful emotional effect (which he misses) but at a compression of sense. He wants to say too much, and the effect is as if some stilted, polemical text had been set to the tune of a sentimental love song.

3.5 ■ Now read again 'The Choirmaster's Burial (p 225), 'The Self-Unseeing' (p 90) and for the first time 'At the Railway Station, Upway' (p 239) and 'During Wind and Rain' (p 226). Make notes on any aspects of these poems that interest you, but pay particular attention to their various metres and the arrangement of the stanzas. Given that all four are short, stanzaic poems, and that each is thematically linked by the references to music, did you feel that these poems had anything else in common?

Discussion

3.6 There is nothing remarkable about the language of 'The Choirmaster's Burial'. Its overall quietness, and a few careful, unobtrusive touches prevent it from becoming that most odious of things, the sentimental proof of God. It is a slight piece, but it

13

takes a certain strength from that common dilemma of the Victorian atheist, who regretted that he could not believe in God because of all the other related reassurances his disbelief closed to him. (Another similar example would be Hardy's justly famous poem 'The Oxen', p 91) Hardy wants to keep just enough ghosts (put another way – a sufficient degree of irrationality) to chide the vicar for his mistaken notions of progress.

3.7 'The Choirmaster's Burial' is perfectly easy to read aloud, which suggests that it is constructed according to a regular metrical pattern. Every line rhymes with one other, though at completely irregular intervals. If you have not already done so, check this out: it makes the poem's neatness and lack of strain more impressive. The lines have between four and seven syllables, again quite irregularly arranged. What makes the poem so strongly metrical is the fact that each line has only two strong stresses: but, again, there is no regularity in their positioning. (Test this for yourself.)

Now most of the pre-twentieth-century poetry that we read is arranged according to quite different metrical principles: the number of syllables to a line is not random, and the stresses form a regular pattern. So what kind (or kinds) of poetry is it that has so effectively habituated us to the sort of metre of 'The Choirmaster's Burial'?

Try this:

    /   /   /   /
Ride a cock-horse to Banbury Cross, (9 syllables)
     /   /   /   /
To see a fine lady ride on a white horse. (11)
   /   /   /   /
Rings on her fingers and bells on her toes (10)
  /   /   /   /
She shall have music where ever she goes. (10)

Or this:

   /   /   /   /
Four and twenty ladies fair (7)
     /   /   /
  Were playing at the ba',   (6)
    /   /   /   /
And out then came the fair Janet, (8)
       /   /   /
  Ance the flower among them a'. (8)

   /   /   /   /
Four and twenty ladies fair, (7)
    /   /   /
  Were playing at the chess, (6)
   /   /   /   /
And out then came the fair Janet (8)
     /   / /
  As green as onie glass. (6)

('The Ballad of Tam Lin')

Stress rhythms are bred in us. Imagine an actor reading a nursery rhyme intelligently for its sense, as he might a Shakespeare speech, and you recognize immediately that in some poetry sense will modify the regular underlying metre, while in other kinds, such as nursery rhymes, ballads, hymns and the metrical arrangements of the psalms and liturgy, stress is allowed to dominate, and form a regular beat. So familiar is the distinction that we are usually able to make it quite automatically. Historically, stress rhythms belong to poetry that was sung or chanted. Most post-medieval and pre-modernist Western music has a regular number of beats to the bar, though there can be almost any number of notes (the equivalent of syllables) in that bar. 'The Choirmaster's Burial' does not look much like a nursery rhyme or a ballad or a hymn, but it makes use of the metrical devices common to all these traditional and popular forms of song.

This poem and 'The Self-Unseeing' both contrast a past that was full of music with a later time that was, or is, by implication silent or at least unmusical. Indeed, 'The Choirmaster's Burial' records a moment of social change of the kind that interested and often saddened Hardy: the vicar decides that 'viols out-of-doors' are old-fashioned. Remember how Hardy's mother felt it better that the children should not be encouraged to like the old folk-dances because they were out-of-date.

3.8 'The Self-Unseeing' apparently records a more intimate regret. He remembers a moment of childhood, enriched by music, the warmth of a fire and a loving family, now dead; and he is saddened because no one recognized the value of the moment as it happened. Yet is it so very personal, after all? Isn't it much more a general reflection on human happiness, with just enough particularization of detail to make it *seem* intimate, and convince us that the poet is sincere – that vital quality which we need in poetry, recognize when we see it, yet are very hard put to define. In fact, details are given very sparingly, almost reticently: we are not told who 'he' and 'she' are, though we guess; we are not told whether anything was being celebrated – whether it was a 'special' occasion; nor are we told that the speaker is revisiting his old home, though I think we infer it. The thinness of narrative need not deter the reader; it can create an intimacy with him because it implies that he already knows, and therefore does not need to be told very much. But if it is thin in narrative specificity, the poem is rich in suggestion. Notice, for example, the skeletal quality of the line 'Footworn and hollowed and thin': the stone flags that were a dancing floor are made to seem almost as dead as the feet that trod them once. 'Footworn' and 'dead feet': the construction is taut, yet marvellously un-obtrusive. In contrast, the last stanza seems full of reflected firelight: the words 'emblazoned' and 'glowed' form a link back to the second stanza

> She sat here in her chair,
> Smiling into the fire.

What is the effect of the alliteration in the third stanza?

This is a question I can seldom answer with any confidence. It is usually easy enough to make up an answer: 'The repeated *x* sounds echo the sense of . . . ' or some such formula. But I am very sceptical about how far sound can echo sense, and certainly that kind of answer will not do here. 'Danced' and 'dream'; 'Blessings' and 'emblazoned'; 'glowed' and 'gleam': it is very obtrusive, but surely it does not reinforce any part of the sense. It does hold each line together, but such short lines are not in much danger of falling apart. So what about this: 'The careful alliteration which holds together the key words of these lines echoes on a purely literal level the close human ties which the poem celebrates.' One has seen worse, but surely it's very incongruous. Much more likely the alliteration has less to do with the sense than with the rhythm. Perhaps it has a slightly naive effect which adds something to the child's perspective, but surely much more important is the way it emphasizes the rhythm. It begins with the word 'dance', and effectively continues the dance

15

rhythm throughout the stanza, because the main stresses fall on the alliterated words.

At first, the metre of 'The Self-Unseeing' seems much more regular than 'The Choirmaster's Burial'. It has three four-line stanzas, each line is felt to be the same length, and there is a strong dactylic impulse about it. (Dactylic: long-short-short.) The opposite of the anapaestic rhythm of 'The Bride-Night Fire' – see para. 2.3. But the lines do not have a regular number of syllables, nor, when you come to test it is the rhythm regularly dactylic:

> Here is the ancient floor,
> Footworn and hollowed and thin,
> Here was the former door
> Where the dead feet walked in.

The first three lines start with a dactyl, but in the first and third lines the second stress is followed by only one unstressed syllable and another stress to close the line. In the fourth line there is plenty of room for argument. I read it as two unstressed syllables, two equal stresses ('dead feet') followed by another but lesser stress ('walked') and an unstressed final syllable. I am fairly certain about 'dead feet' but I can see that the third stress could be on 'Where' or even 'in'. The line could just about be said with four stressed syllables, though they could not all be equal.

The first line of the second stanza can also be stressed in different ways. 'Here' and 'chair' must have a stress, and the line asks for a third somewhere – but on 'she' (because 'He' in the third line is certainly stressed) or on 'sat'? In the second line 'Smiling into the fire' the first and last syllables are stressed, and a third, lesser stress surely falls on 'in': / x / x x /. The third line is emphatically / x / x /, and the fourth may be / x x / x x /, depending on how consistently you pronounce 'higher' and whether with one syllable or two.

The third stanza is completely regular, unlike the first and second. Each line has the same number of syllables. Notice again how the stresses fall on the alliterated syllables.

> Childlike, I danced in a dream;   / x x / x x /
> Blessings emblazoned that day;   / x x / x x /
> Everything glowed with a gleam;   / x x / x x /
> Yet we were looking away!   / x x / x x /

If it is to be worth doing, this kind of analysis needs to be done slowly.

The exercises in these first sections have not been introduced for Hardy's sake alone, but to help you with work in the later parts of the course. The practice on metre that you put in here will certainly not be wasted, for even the freest verse form has some kind of metrical basis.

3.9 I find 'The Self-Unseeing' a very moving poem, whereas I find 'At the Railway Station, Upway' only touching. This, one feels, is a distinction that Hardy himself was aware of. He saw (or possibly only imagined) the incident, sensed that there was something in it, and recorded it. He did not try too hard to define or emphasize what that something was. Perhaps any incident involving music would attract him. Sentimentality is a matter of individual taste, but I think Hardy is seldom guilty of over-exploiting or indulging himself in the sentimental potential of a subject. Nor is he abashed by it. There is nothing embarrassing in a poem like this: it keeps cool. Very faint praise perhaps, but it is surely not a poem that expects a grand response either way.

Once again, the experienced story-teller is in evidence. Hardy begins his poem somewhere near the heart of his anecdote. Again, there is the clarity that Pound admired, and the point is made with perfect lucidity, using prose words in a prose order. All that is artful in the piece is its metre, and that is rich indeed. It might seem over-rich were it not in such perfect accord with the ordinary inflections of the sentences. No distortion, not even the faintest pressure is necessary to make the sense comply with the metrical arrangement. It is possible to spend a great deal of time trying to find a formula for the metrical pattern that one feels so strongly, but it is difficult to produce anything satisfying. As in 'The Self-Unseeing' it is not always possible to be sure which syllables are stressed. Then variations in pace cannot be separated from the effects of the metre: for example, the poem slows a little at the third line. The rhymes too are very important (a b c d d a b / c a e e f f f g g d d). None of the first four lines rhyme with each other, then suddenly the fifth line rhymes with the fourth. This creates a sudden expectation of coherence, which is fulfilled as a b and c are rhymed in due order. Is this really what happens as we read? And what is the effect of the break between b and c?

Another a rhyme suggests the sequence is about to begin again, but instead come new rhymes, in pairs and one quick triplet, which emphasizes the grim irony of the convict's song. The final couplet rhymes with the only couplet in the first part of the pattern: the two pairs of lines have so many words in common that they are almost a refrain. Perhaps this cannot be called a pattern, but it has certainly been carefully planned. The work that has gone into it, however, is left to make its effects very quietly. At a normal reading it would never be spotted. Perhaps this is what is meant when critics call Hardy a craftsman. Sometimes he puts infinite skill and patience into carving heads on cherry stones.

3.10 There is no waste of skill in 'During Wind and Rain'. Its construction is as perfect as anything Hardy ever achieved. Music is mentioned in only one of its stanzas – the first. But the whole poem is very like a song. Here, as with many of Hardy's lyrics, you half hear music as you say it, and wonder whether he did not have some specific tune in mind. Especially song-like are the refrain-lines, and the last lines of each stanza, which suggest a modulation in a minor key like the elaborate tonic effects of many Victorian song settings. The moments the poem recalls seem to be almost random, yet the first certainly helps to suggest how the rest should be read.

3.11 The poem has four stanzas, all constructed alike. The first five lines of each describe a typical moment of family life; then there is a refrain line, varied slightly in alternate stanzas. Each stanza ends with a longer line which (except in the case of the final line) does not refer to the people at all. Instead the first three final lines describe quickly but vividly something in the natural but non-human world which is in contrast to the mood of each opening section. The last line of all is the only one which unmistakably implies that they – anonymous, friendly, familiar ghosts – are dead:

Down their carved names the rain-drop ploughs.

The suggestion of death is contained only in the words 'carved names', and it is only faintly chilling. Yet everything seems to have foreshadowed this line.

So we have discovered that each stanza is divided into two parts by a refrain: in the first and third stanzas the line

Ah, no; the years O!

And in the second and fourth,

Ah, no; the years, the years;

This variation in the refrain helps us realize that there is in fact another refrain line, the second in each stanza. But in this case it is the *sense* that is repeated not the words. The first and last stanzas have almost identical lines

He, she, all of them – yea

He, she all of them – aye

But the other two corresponding lines are quite differently worded, though 'yea' and 'aye' alternate regularly.

Elders and juniors – aye

Men and maidens – yea

Each of these four lines suggest a family, or a natural, domestic random group of people, of different sexes and ages. And each time the line ends with an affirmative. But that affirmative, in the living human part of each stanza, is cancelled by the negative which is in the refrain dividing the opening from the quite different mood of the final line.

Ah, no; the years, the years.

I think we should be hard put to describe exactly what the words aye, yea and no *mean* in this poem, or to define their place in the syntax. They represent affirmation and negation of an unspecific absolute kind.

Now it may be that the first time you read 'During Wind and Rain' you were puzzled by it. Not because a single word or phrase is obscure, but because it is not immediately obvious how the parts are related. There is also the same rather baffling lack of particularity combined with vividness of detail that characterized 'The Self-Unseeing'. The construction of the poem helps us to understand it. 'Yes' is cancelled out by 'no' and the years, and we understand that each final line belongs to the 'no' and not the 'yes' that has gone for good. Doubtless there are more elegant ways of putting what I have just said, but what Hardy can do so beautifully and economically in poetry is difficult to express in prose. The relation of the parts of each stanza to one another is not made clear by the familiar progressive connections of prose syntax, but once again by techniques more common in ballad and song. Unless some prejudice exists, the human mind is generally willing to connect things where only the most minimal relationship is apparent. Take away the refrain lines and you may not feel you are losing much sense. But without their gentle unobtrusive guidance the reader would instinctively incorporate each seventh line into the scene which precedes. It might be awkward, but it would not be impossible to discover a connection: the sick leaves of the first stanza could be seen as the inhospitable out-doors from which the singers are protected. Indeed, despite the refrains, the possibility of this kind of connection remains. But when the years and the denial intervene the relationship is painfully stretched, and we recognize the vast and all-important distance between the two parts of each stanza.

Rhyme and rhythm are also meaningful parts of the construction. Each stanza is rhymed a b c b c d a. Rhymes a and c are peculiar to their respective stanzas; b is the same rhyme throughout the poem – if you accept that aye and yea rhyme with each other. So the first and last lines of each stanza are held together by rhyme, thus emphasizing the contrast. And each second line, the semi-refrain line, rhymes with the shortest fourth line of each stanza which is part of the anecdotal first section. This has the effect of emphasizing the continuity. Each of the four distinct memories hands on a rhyme to the next stanza, thus (stanza 1) yea – play, (2) aye – gay, (3) yea – bay, (4) aye – day.

The rhythm of 'During Wind and Rain' is broadly iambic, though the number of syllables in the corresponding lines of each stanza varies. Again, the regulating factor is the number of stresses. Each first line has three stresses:

> They sing their dearest songs (6 syllables)   x / x / x /
>
> They clear the creeping moss (6)   x / x / x /
>
> They are blithely breakfasting all (8)   x x / x / x x /
>
> They change to a high new house (7)   x / x x / x /

And each last line, which you will remember rhymes with the first, has more syllables and one more stress. Each stanza is underlined by a longer, heavier line than those preceding. The final lines quite literally impart a kind of gravity.

Look at each fourth line:

> And one to play
>
> And the garden gay
>
> With a glimpse of the bay
>
> On the lawn all day

How many syllables and how many stresses does each of these lines have? What is their effect when considered in context? How do the effects of rhythm combine with the rhyme properties of the lines?

This is laborious work and I do not want to prolong it. Yet I suspect that perhaps more than any other poet, Hardy might have been pleased by this kind of analysis. The complexity of structural pattern in this poem is staggering, yet how unobtrusive. We remember that Hardy was trained as an architect, and like all architects of his time, he was particularly interested in the principles of the gothic style. In some medieval cathedrals, by some miracle of skill, stone seems lighter than air. But Hardy knew that such effects were not achieved miraculously at all, but by the application of the laws of physics. As a practical man, Hardy was not at all the kind of sentimentalist who felt that the effect of a thing might be spoiled if you knew how it was made. I rather suspect he might feel you ought to know how it was made. ■

3.12   This section has run an apparently devious course. It began with a simple bio-graphical account of Hardy's affection for old-fashioned music, then took in some discussion of his use of different metres, and concluded with a look at some of the more technical aspects of his constructions. I have had in mind an analogy with the musician's art which I do not want to take too far for fear of the usual traps which beset such comparisons. Hardy, I want to suggest, is not so much a musical, as a *musician-like* poet. Indeed, not all his poetry is perfectly pleasing to the ear. But there is a kind of half-secret workmanship in many of his poems which reminds me of the musical laws by which composers agree to bind themselves. The untutored listener may not understand how the unity of a piece of music is achieved, though he may sense its effect. And a poem by Hardy may appear to have been effortlessly made, until a careful scrutiny reveals the strictness of the rules by which he has worked.

4 THE COUNTRYSIDE

4.1 The life and work of rural England is a major theme in Hardy's novels. He was particularly aware of the changes that increasing industrialization and mechanization were bringing to a way of life previously hardly altered over centuries. On the whole, he regretted what he saw. He welcomed, of course, improvements in health and education, and the growing independence and comparative prosperity of the agricultural labourers; but he was also saddened by the decline of old customs and the reckless abandonment of ancient traditions. We have already noticed in his poetry a deep regret for a past richer than the present. Yet this sadness for what is gone, is conditioned by a practical, realistic sense that the present must be lived through. The countryside is not as large a presence in the poetry as it is in the novels, though many critics misled by *The Woodlanders* or *Tess of the D'Urbervilles* or simply by the semi-mythic fame of Hardy's Wessex have persisted in believing that he is, above all, a poet of rural life. Creighton, for example says

> The mysterious relation between nature and man, the numinous but indif-
> ferent, the lovely, inscrutable, untrustworthy, evolutionarily destructive but
> in some contradictory sense almost mystically significant, face of nature,
> have a place on nearly every page he wrote. (Creighton Introduction p ix.)

4.2 This is surely an overstatement. Creighton's own first section, *Nature and Man* is very short. In it there are a few things that remind one of some of the most famous descriptive passages in the novels. Read 'Ice on the Highway' (p 13), 'Throwing a Tree' (p 20), 'A Sheep Fair' (p 7) and 'Last Look Round St Martin's Fair' (p 9).

The first two are almost pure description, with only the faintest trace of authorial pressure towards a specific emotion. 'Ice on the Highway' describes something so commonplace that it hardly seems worth recording. The reader is pushed (though not very hard) by words like 'trudge', 'perforce', 'must', 'whether or no', but the endurance these words recognize is of a very commonplace kind. (Who does not sometimes have to go shopping in the cold?) 'Throwing a Tree' is a fine example of how pre-eminently aware Hardy was of the importance of knowing how to do things. Indeed, the description of how the tree is felled is of much more interest than the emotional weighting introduced by words like 'executioners', 'death-mark' and the last line. After all, one does not need an exceptional sensibility to recognize that felling a mature tree is always a melancholy business. And most of the poem is uncluttered by obtrusive manipulations of this kind. Hardy's impulse in both these instances seems to have been simply to describe something he had observed; but some strange sense of duty seems to have impelled him to make each poem take on at least a modicum of moral responsibility. Of the two impulses, that which led him to describe is the more interesting and makes for finer poetry. Hardy said remarkably little about his motives in writing, but it seems a reasonable guess that it was his acute sense of gradual loss in a changing world that made him want to record the things he observed.

Certainly the first two stanzas of 'A Sheep Fair' are valuable for the clarity of the observation and for the underlying conviction that such an event was worth recording. Every reader is surely convinced that this is indeed a life-like account of such a fair, and even if such truth to life is not high on the scale of exclusively literary priorities, it is of value to that part of the human spirit which likes to recognize the ties that link past and present.

The Postscript is another matter, and the poem would be better without it. What possible merit is there in saying that the auctioneer who said going-going so often is now himself gone? Every auctioneer that is born of woman must eventually fall under the hammer. As in the two previous poems, description alone did not satisfy Hardy. 'A Sheep Fair' concludes with that characteristic acknowledgement that time will bring about sequel and change.

'Last Look Round St Martin's Fair' is probably the least successful of these four poems. Its awkwardness is redeemed in patches by the interest of what is recorded, but the note of melancholy is obsessive. I do not object particularly to the weariness of 'The woman in red, at the nut-stall with the gun', but there is something faintly absurd about the note of doom in the following couplet:

> The unsold heathcroppers are driven home
> To the shades of the Great Forest whence they come

Nothing in the poem indicates why such gloomy portentousness should be appropriate, unless it is the approach of night and winter. The passing of daylight and the changing seasons frequently remind men of their own transience, of course, but here they seem to signal some more universal dissolution without carrying much conviction that it is really imminent.

4.3 Two fine poems in this section, 'I am the One' (p 17) and 'Afterwards' (p 18) record without diffidence Hardy's consciousness of the intimacy he enjoyed with the things of the countryside. But he seems to have been unconscious of any bias in his interpretations of what he saw. It is not good enough to say simply that Hardy looked at the black side of things. But it is generally true that when events or phenomena offer an optimistic interpretation of themselves, then he is surprised, and asks how this can be. He seems to feel that from bad to worse is the inevitable way of the world.

Look at 'The Year's Awakening' (p 2), 'At Middle-field Gate in February' (p 2), 'A Backward Spring' (p 3), 'I Watched a Blackbird' (p 4), 'Proud Songsters' (p 4), 'An Unkindly May' (p 4), 'An August Midnight' (p 6). 'At Day-Close in November' (p 11), 'Winter in Durnover Field' (p 13), 'The Darkling Thrush' (p 14) and 'Before and After Summer' (p 16).

4.4 'The Darkling Thrush' appeared in *The Times* of 1 January 1900. Donald Davie is very sceptical about it:

> A modern enthusiast for the poem, John Berryman, makes much of the
> irony latent in the last line:
>
> > Some blessed Hope, whereof he knew
> >   And I was unaware.
>
> (That is to say, the hope is an illusion.) But can we doubt that the reader of
> *The Times* in 1900, and the readers of the anthologies ever since and at
> present, read the lines quite differently, to mean: 'I, the notorious pessimist
> and author of *Jude the Obscure*, humbly confess myself foolish beside the

sanguine and resolute wisdom of this bird'? And – a nastier question – can we doubt that Hardy, either when he wrote the poem for this occasion or else when he mailed it to *The Times* to meet the occasion, counted upon the editor and the regular readers of the newspaper to take it in just that up-beat, unexceptional way? Such are the dishonesties, or the opportunities for dishonesty which attend a poet who, like Hardy, declares that his highest ambition is to place one or two poems in an anthology like The Golden Treasury. (Davie *Thomas Hardy and British Poetry* p 38.)

But here is a third way, which is neither Berryman's nor Davie's, and that is to take it as an absolutely straight account of the contradictory evidences that nature affords. As is usual with Hardy, the observation is painstaking, the recording carefully precise:

> The tangled bine-stems scored the sky
>   Like strings of broken lyres

And as usual, Hardy is meticulous about saying no more than he means:

> The ancient pulse of germ and birth
>   Was shrunken hard and dry,
> And every spirit upon earth
>   Seemed fervourless as I.

Seemed, not was. Such care produces at least the effect of honesty. Nothing around him suggests an optimistic prognostication; yet the thrush, who is part of the bleakness

> Had chosen thus to fling his soul
>   Upon the growing gloom.

'Chosen' is important, though it should not be taken to imply that Hardy has anthropomorphized the bird. The caution persists: Hardy only says he *could* think, and not that he believes the bird has access to information not available to him. The question is, quite simply, why should the bird sing, against all the evidence? Surely it is better to leave the question in its simple form, and not try to interpret it as either cynicism or irony. Not that such qualities were not part of Hardy's make-up. But it is equally fair to say that he was not a very sophisticated thinker, though perhaps he thought he was. He was never abashed by the naivety of his own thoughts and impulses. Look for example at 'An August Midnight' (p 6).

4.5 'They know Earth-secrets that know not I.' Hardy's earnestness of purpose is such that he is uninhibited by the clumsiness of his order. It is too much to say that he is overwhelmed by awe in the face of nature's mysteries. What comes across is much more like honest bafflement. In 'I Watched a Blackbird' the lovingly observed detail suggests that Hardy recognizes a confident purposiveness in nature but does not understand it. The hesitation implied in the words 'As if' is vital. What makes the bird so sure? The same words recur in 'Proud Songsters'. All time is not theirs; soon they will be earth, air and rain again; and so, why sing? It seems that temperamentally Hardy could not understand the classical response, *carpe diem*, seize the day. As I said before, for him every action, every moment had its sequel, of which he was always conscious. And perhaps because for the individual life the sequel in the end is always death he tended to interpret the larger rhythms not as a constant circle, but as a spiral, downwards. 'The Year's Awakening' and 'A Backward Spring' both evince the same bewilderment. The vital, positive activity of nature's humbler creatures is irrational and unfathomable when measured against the evidence of purpose that she presents to the senses and intellect of man. Many poets have leaned heavily on what is called the pathetic fallacy, seeing in the changing face of nature a reflection of the human condition. But from the infinite correspondences available, Hardy makes a very partial selection. In human life summer is always followed by winter; only amongst animals, birds and the silent roots is winter succeeded by spring. The American critic, John Crowe Ransom in the *Southern Review* says that Hardy celebrates mortality 'and the ignominious ending of those who once were quick and beautiful . . . [he is] extremely ingenious and experienced in catching fresh perceptions of this brutal fact'. Sometimes the relish Hardy finds in mortality is macabre: remember 'Ah, are you digging on my grave?' quoted in Unit 1, para. 2.11?

4.6 Though the arrangement in the set book is useful in that it brings together poems with similar subjects and thus helps the reader organize his response to what can seem a hopelessly fragmented and disorderly poetic achievement, it is also dangerous in that it suggests a kind of rigid docketing: if a poem is one thing, it cannot be another. Hardy's poems about the countryside contain many exquisite and moving observations. But when we read so many with so much in common close together, it becomes clear that the countryside was not a pastoral refuge for Hardy: despite its beauty, it was more a place of confrontation. With the evidence of the eternal cycles of the countryside before him, Hardy faces up to his own mortality. And many poems, not just in this group, but throughout his poetical works, evince an unmistakable note of satisfaction which comes from having confronted the inevitable ending without losing his nerve. This is, of course, the supreme challenge to the atheist, and Hardy seems to have felt a continuing necessity to test his atheism against the brutal fact of death. Atheism does not preclude optimism, but it gives it impassable limits. Above all, it sets the finite human consciousness against the seemingly infinite repetitions of the rest of nature. Strongly influenced by post-Darwinian currents, Hardy may have felt that birds could afford to be cheerful as long as their species survived, whereas to human beings what matters is the survival of the self and a handful of other cherished, individual minds. For the most part, he could confront mortality with a spring in his step – look again at 'At Day-close in November'. But in constantly making himself face up to the worst he was sometimes overwhelmed by it. No poet gives a more convincing account of depression. Read the three parts of 'In Tenebris' (pp 116–18). (The title means 'In Darkness'.) For obvious reasons, they may seem a digression in a section of the unit entitled *The Countryside*. But I want to make it clear once for all that the sadness one so frequently encounters in Hardy's poetry is not simply a melancholia induced by the countryside, though I think that its roots may well lie in his long contemplation of the relationship between man and nature. Hardy has frequently been called a pessimist – a charge which he denied hotly and a word which I have deliberately avoided. Such blanket definitions are ultimately evasions. But there is no doubt that Hardy wrote some very powerful poems about the bleakest moments in life. In fact, the three moods of the 'In Tenebris' poems are quite different: but they share an almost absolute depth of despondency.

4.7 There is a morbidity about Hardy's mood in these three poems which probably most of us would recognize. The three poems actually describe three different states of mind, in spite of having the same title. The most important thing they have in common is their pitch of dejection, but there are other similarities. All three are spotted with self-pity, something we have all been taught to despise. It has been said that Hardy's poetry often brings the critic to the absurd position where he must praise its faults. Usually the faults meant are stylistic. But here the self-pity does not make us reject the poems as ignobly maudlin. It makes them more terrible, because absolutely convincing.

4.8 The 'In Tenebris' poems were first published in 1901, in a collection which included Hardy's ironic reflections on the Boer War (these are discussed in the next section of these units). 'In Tenebris' must have seemed then rather un-British, unpatriotic. The second, least personal of the poems in particular attacks precisely those public declarations of manly, preposterous optimism which played such a large part in English life around the turn of the century, and which even found its expression in highly popular poetry – see Stead *The New Poetic*, and Unit 1.

> Breezily go they, breezily come; their dust smokes around their career,
> Till I think I am one born out of due time, who has no calling here.

There is no evasion in Hardy's poetry. His characteristic attitude is a kind of un-aggressive confrontation. He does not fight life, but he faces it without blinking:

> Twice no one dies.

This quality in Hardy must not be mistaken for stoicism: there is no patient, un-complaining endurance. What is constantly amazing is the coolness with which he faces the worst life can bring him. There is complaint, of course; but who apart from Hardy has set out to define his grief? In the extract from his book on Hardy reprinted in the Course Reader, Douglas Brown makes an interesting comparison with Tennyson. Brown suggests that there is something contrived about Tennyson's famous 'In Memoriam' – a sequence of poems mourning the death of a friend. The effect of the poems has been calculated to move the reader to feel grief. It is worth asking whether Hardy's prime aim was to move his reader to grief, or whether first of all he wanted to set down a record of his own grief, and in fact cared very little for arousing intense emotion in his reader.

5 WAR – THE PUBLIC WORLD

5.1 The Boer War began when Hardy was nearly sixty; and when the Great War broke out he was an old man. There is no useful distinction to be made between his responses to the two wars. He had been very much an amateur historian of war; he had only informal, social contacts with military men; and he was far too old for active service. His poems speak from a distance, and both his pity and his ironically expressed horror, though profound, are without the passion of a personal involvement. These qualities are all the more noticeable because of course the greatest, and most famous poetry of the First World War was written by the young men who fought it, and who were, many of them, involved to the cost of their lives. Nevertheless, Hardy's war poetry is not negligible. Creighton's selection is short, and you should read all of it, on pp 180–90 of your anthology.

5.2 I said that there is little point in separating the First World War poems from the Boer War pieces. Perhaps this is most clearly justified by the history of one of the most well-known of Hardy's poems: 'In Time of "The Breaking of Nations"'. Hardy said in the *Life* that it 'contains a feeling that moved me in 1870, during the Franco-Prussian war, when I chanced to be looking at such an agricultural incident in Cornwall. But I did not write the verses until the war with Germany of 1914, and onwards.' What was important to Hardy was the things that make all wars alike, and not the historical, political, geographical or technological factors that make them different. But none of the greatest poetry inspired by the First World War was political in the narrow sense of taking sides. It is worth comparing Hardy's poem 'The Man he Killed' with Wilfred Owen's famous and far more profound poem 'Strange Meeting'.

Strange Meeting

It seemed that out of battle I escaped
Down some profound dull tunnel, long since scooped
Through granites which titanic wars had groined.
Yet also there encumbered sleepers groaned,
Too fast in thought or death to be bestirred.
Then, as I probed them, one sprang up, and stared
With piteous recognition in fixed eyes,
Lifting distressful hands as if to bless.
And by his smile I knew that sullen hall,
By his dead smile I knew we stood in Hell.
With a thousand pains that vision's face was grained;
Yet no blood reached there from the upper ground,
And no guns thumped, or down the flues made moan.
'Strange friend,' I said, 'here is no cause to mourn.'
'None,' said the other, 'save the undone years,
The hopelessness. Whatever hope is yours,
Was my life also; I went hunting wild
After the wildest beauty in the world,
Which lies not calm in eyes, or braided hair,
But mocks the steady running of the hour,
And if it grieves, grieves richlier than here.
For by my glee might many men have laughed,
And of my weeping something had been left,
Which must die now. I mean the truth untold,
The pity of war, the pity war distilled.
Now men will go content with what we spoiled.
Or, discontent, boil bloody, and be spilled.
They will be swift with the swiftness of the tigress,
None will break ranks, though nations trek from progress.
Courage was mine, and I had mystery,
Wisdom was mine, and I had mastery;
To miss the march of this retreating world
Into vain citadels that are not walled.
Then, when much blood had clogged their chariot-wheels
I would go up and wash them from sweet wells,
Even with truths that lie too deep for taint.
I would have poured my spirit without stint
But not through wounds; not on the cess of war.
Foreheads of men have bled where no wounds were.
I am the enemy you killed, my friend.
I knew you in this dark; for so you frowned
Yesterday through me as you jabbed and killed.
I parried; but my hands were loath and cold.
Let us sleep now . . . '

5.3 ■ There is no doubt that Hardy's poem is the lesser of the two and to suggest the comparison would have been fatuous, were it not that 'The Man he Killed' (like

25

so much of Hardy's poetry that is not quite among his best) has a curious wiry resilience. It is a poem that can stand on its own terms, and it is able to do so because it seems to know precisely what those terms are. A colloquial phrase, in its fullest sense, seems appropriate here: Hardy always seemed to know what he was about.

The climactic line of Owen's magnificent poem is

> I am the enemy you killed, my friend.

This paradoxical closeness of enemy and friend is also the theme of Hardy's poem. It is worth asking whether there is anything the shorter poem includes that the longer one lacks.

Discussion

5.4   No one has ever been fiercer than Owen in denouncing 'The old lie: Dulce et Decorum est/Pro patria mori.' (It is sweet and right to die for one's country.) His work will be discussed again more extensively in Units 4–5 and I do not want to anticipate too much here. But the comparison is useful because it makes clear things that otherwise might take some time to define. Place these two poems side by side and we can see at once that the fine, high tone of Owen's poem excludes the common-place; at the same time it becomes clearer that Hardy's decision to avoid rhetoric, heroism and all but the most mediocre movements of the imagination was also a deliberate act of excision. I do not mean to imply that Owen lacked sympathy for the men of the ranks. 'Strange Meeting' is not a realistic poem; it does not address itself to Owen's fellow soldiers, but to his fellow poets. Or rather, it addresses all men as if they were his fellow poets. It is a very Romantic stance – a tendency also suggested by the splendid absence of particularity in the strange friend's speech. When a poet is as elusive as Hardy it may help to try and define by opposites. In Hardy you find tacit hints of a rather irritable impatience with writing like this:

> I went hunting wild
> After the wildest beauty in the world,
> Which lies not calm in eyes, or braided hair
> But mocks the steady running of the hour,
> And if it grieves, grieves richlier than here.

The practical, no-nonsense (and sometimes very annoying) streak in Hardy would never have let him leave his readers in suspense of his meaning for so long, even if he had to invent words or bend the English syntax to breaking point to do it.

5.5   Hardy was always divided by his social and intellectual aspirations and the instincts of his birth. Yet his novels and poetry are packed with characters and incidents from working-class life unspoiled by condescension, their clarity undimmed by their author's success. The term 'working-class' is particularly appropriate in Hardy's case: no novelists before him and few since have been as aware of the fact that most of the waking hours of most men are filled with work. In war time a man was as likely to enlist because he was out of work as for any patriotic sentiment.

> He thought he'd 'list, perhaps
> Off-hand like – just as I –
> Was out of work – had sold his traps –
> No other reason why.

26

Hardy was, of course, not the only poet to understand that most of the men who fight and die in war are as commonplace as his speaker here.[5] But no one in his time was as single-minded, as consistent and truly sympathetic in honouring the debts of all warring nations to their unknown soldiers. The better-known poetry of the First World War is of different kinds; even where it most furiously debunks the phoney glamorization of war it expresses half a regret for the dead chivalry it knew perfectly well had always been a fiction. Owen is horrified, and expresses his horror brutally at times. But he also gives the impression that learning the awful truth has saddened him. But Hardy, who never came close to a war himself, can write as if he never had any illusions. And it is this quality of being without illusions that makes the best of his war poetry seem particularly 'modern'. Indeed, whereas in most of his poetry there is very little which ostensibly connects it with the times in which it was written, war poetry like this seems 'advanced'; its severe factuality and anti-heroic bias looks like a reaction to Edwardian jingoism. And despite Hardy's distance from the fighting (he did not even suffer the loss of a close relative) 'The Man he Killed' seems curiously authentic. ∎

5.6   The Great War itself produced a mass of popular poetry which was certainly in the broadside tradition, not least because it generally parodied well-known songs of the day and used their tunes. John Press says:

> It was, perhaps, the common soldiers who first apprehended the horror and suffering of the war in their full intensity. The British Army kept its class-structure largely unimpaired throughout the war, and the officers, thanks partly to their privileged and responsible positions, saw the conflict in a more heroic light than the other ranks. Almost from the start the 'tommies' improvised verses which are likely to be remembered as the last authentic folk-poetry to be composed by Englishmen.[6] A. J. P. Taylor, in his magnificent historical narrative, has described the nature of these songs: 'The tunes were usually adapted from contemporary music-hall "hits". The words were self-depreciatory and often obscene. No other army has ever gone to war, proclaiming its own incompetence and reluctance to fight, and no army has fought better. The humble Englishman found his voice, and these songs preserve him for posterity.'[7] But precisely because they were the rough, genuine, obscene songs of the trenches they did not reach the ears of the literate men and women living snug at home.
> (Press *A Map of Modern English Verse* pp 135–6.)

It might seem that Hardy, in poems like 'The Man he Killed' could have been the humble Englishman's spokesman, but without his rough, genuine obscenity. So can we classify Hardy as an anti-war poet, and therefore one of the 'advanced' party? Donald Davie challenges such a simple point of view:

> . . . we realize how disarming Hardy is when we see ['Drummer Hodge'] esteemed by some who would castigate Rupert Brooke's '1914', though the senselessness of war is glossed over by the same means in the one poem as in the other. Similarly, though John Crowe Ransom was right to reprove the reader who thought 'Channel Firing'[8] was mere sabre-rattling, it is disingenuous to remember this poem and 'In Time of "The Breaking of

[5]Compare Owen's attempt to impersonate the common soldier, printed on p 152 of John Press's *A Map of Modern English Verse*. And of course Kipling should not be forgotten.

[6]But what about football and rugby songs? Pickets' chants? The new street songs of Northern Ireland?

[7]A. J. P. Taylor *English History 1919–45*, p 62.

[8]Creighton, p 218.

Nations"'", while forgetting several other poems by Hardy that are indeed sabre-rattlings or morale-builders or worse. (Davie *Thomas Hardy and British Poetry* p 36.)

5.7 It is worth following his argument in detail. The Brooke poem Davie refers to is this famous sonnet:

> If I should die, think only this of me:
>   That there's some corner of a foreign field
> That is for ever England. There shall be
>   In that rich earth a richer dust concealed;
> A dust which England bore, shaped, made aware,
>   Gave, once, her flowers to love, her ways to roam,
> A body of England's breathing English air,
>   Washed by the rivers, blest by suns of home.
> And think, this heart, all evil shed away,
>   A pulse in the eternal mind, no less
>   Gives somewhere back the thoughts by England given;
> Her sights and sounds; dreams happy as her day;
>   And laughter, learnt of friends; and gentleness,
>   In hearts at peace, under an English heaven.

■ Is it fair to say that this poem and 'Drummer Hodge' both gloss over 'the sense-lessness of war' in the same way?

Discussion

5.8 Well, perhaps Drummer Hodge has made some corner of the veldt forever England, but really I think there is even less similarity between 'Drummer Hodge' and '1914' than between 'The Man he Killed' and 'Strange Meeting'. In Brooke's poem the brutal fact that a dead body mingles with the earth in which it lies is transfigured, and made to express the loftiest, purest feelings of patriotic love. In Hardy's poem the same brutal fact is rendered bearable not by idealism, but according to the laws of nature. In another poem Hardy wrote:

> Portion of this yew
> Is a man my grandsire knew,
> Bosomed here at its foot:
> This branch may be his wife,
> A ruddy human life
> Now turned to a green shoot.

('Transformations')

Again, Hardy is confronting life, not trying to make it more acceptable by self-deceptive sophistries of the will. Brooke's poem is dated, because it implies a world and a way of life gone for ever. And it is sentimental, because it invests enormous emotive power in a view of life that is on examination, very small and narrow. It is difficult to imagine Brooke putting himself in the place of a German soldier dying in France. But it is possible to imagine Hardy writing a poem about, say, an African slave dying in Europe, and this is because England, in 'Drummer Hodge', is a less important concept than *home*. You may smile slightly at 'foreign constellations' and 'His homely Northern breast' and feel that Hardy's heart is in Wessex (where else could it be?) but the stress is not on the virtues of England, but how far Hodge is from home. Brooke tries, heroically, to turn death into life – look at the first three lines of the sestet. The pathos lies partly in the effort, but more in the sweetness of the England conjured up: it actually invites the reader to imagine what he would miss if he were dead. There is no such conventional heroism in Hardy's factual assessment of the life that follows death. But in contrast to this stern rationality, the pathos lies in the suggestion that Hodges' ghost will be a long way from home – for a ghost of some kind, however dim, is implied by the insistence that it will somehow matter that 'strange-eyed constellations' should watch over him. When Brooke thinks of what will happen after death he sees a summer's day in England, spent with friends of his own class; Hardy, on the other hand, measures the pain of the soldier's death by the distance between his home, and the unknown constellations of another hemisphere. What is for Brooke a kind of consolation, is for Hardy an additional poignancy. ■

5.9 If you read the appropriate chapters in Press and Stead you will see that the reactions of poets to the Great War fell into two almost completely distinct and unreconcilable kinds. There was the patriotic, stirring poetry of acceptance and, much more highly thought of today, the poetry of protest. There is nothing difficult to understand here. Surely the Great War was so vital a theme that men who decided to write about it would feel compelled to put their ideas in order, to make up their minds about it. Pacifist or combatant, surely every thinking person must have had a political attitude to the war. When we begin to read Hardy's poems about war we imagine that here at last must be a subject that will reveal something about his opinions. And Creighton's selection may have made you feel that although 'protest' might be too energetic a word to use of Hardy's war poetry, nevertheless he was a poet of grumbling, unwilling resignation.

5.10 Yet Davie is right to remind his readers of 'several other poems by Hardy that are . . . sabre-rattling or morale-builders or worse'. Early in the war Hardy wrote a poem which contains the following stanza:

> In our heart of hearts believing
>> Victory crowns the just,
>> And that braggarts must
>> Surely bite the dust,
> Press we to the field ungrieving,
> In our heart of hearts believing
>> Victory crowns the just.

('Men who March Away')

Later, he wrote the following sonnet, dated March 1917.

> Up and be doing all who have a hand
> To lift, a back to bend. It must not be
> In times like these that vaguely linger we
> To air our vaunts and hopes; and leave our land
>
> Untended as a wild of weeds and sand.
> – Say, then, 'I come!' and go, O women and men
> Of palace, ploughshare, easel, counter, pen;
> That scareless, scathless, England may still stand.
>
> Would years but let me stir as once I stirred
> At many a dawn to take the forward track,
> And with a stride plunged on to enterprize,
>
> I now would speed like yester wind that whirred
> Through yielding pines; and serve with never a slack,
> So loud for promptness all around outcries!

29

■ You cannot call this empty rhetoric, because it does put fire of a kind in the belly. But there is something hollow and ghastly about it. Compare the much quieter, but far more profoundly disturbing poem 'I looked up from my writing' (p 188).

Discussion

5.11 This surely is the heart of the matter: a passionate, but inactive state of guilt. Here is a statement of the paradox, even if it could hardly be called an explanation of why Hardy was apparently able to write for both sides (the pro- and anti-war factions) with equal conviction. Remember 'Valenciennes': Corporal Tullidge had earned the best right in the world to loathe war, yet he still had a kind of zest for fighting. This poem has no lust for battle. It describes a state of sickened inaction, the mortal guilt of passive connivance. If it is about the uselessness of art, then it is self-disproving, even though it does not vindicate

> the blinkered mind
> Of one who wants to write a book
> In a world of such a kind.

Nor is it the poem of a man who is uninvolved simply because he is too old – a man who hears the distant battle, but does not feel it. His senses are so alert to pain that they are roused by the touch of moonlight. Creighton has put this poem in a sub-section entitled 'War', but is it really a 'war' poem at all? Isn't what is of universal application in this poem more important than the specific reference to an unspecified war? Isn't the real subject of this poem the continuing dilemma of any well-to-do society? The style of this poem is very vulnerable; what makes it powerful is the way it searches out the tender spots in the conscience of – say – someone who sometimes feels that writing about poetry is not what the world needs. ■

Hardy's poems often face the reader with strange problems of size and scale. Here his subject is ostensibly a tiny incident in a major catastrophe. Yet really it is about something that is even bigger than the war itself.

5.12 Look at 'Channel Firing' (p 218), written just before the outbreak of war, though surely it could have been included in Creighton's 'War' section. God is chatting with grim amiability to the lazy companionable dead. At first it seems little more than a sardonic little ghost story. But notice how Hardy stretches its implications. The last two lines are powerfully evocative. The phrase 'As far inland' seems to act like a paraphrase of something referring to distances in time: Stourton Tower – the Middle Ages and unceasing war; Camelot – Arthur's idealism dissolved in blood; and starlit Stonehenge – butchery in the name of religion. It is these very lightly-made connections between war and religion which should take us to the point it is very easy to miss: that God himself is not much better than any of his generations. Hardy believed that men had made God in their own image.

5.13 Is it possible to feel some sympathy with such diverse points of view – to hate war and yet write poems to boost recruitment figures? The long perspective of 'Channel Firing' suggests that Hardy, the immemorial onlooker, would not sacrifice anything of the breadth of his vision for any kind of partisanship, no matter how good the cause. Differences, even extreme opposites, have a right to exist and be acknowledged. And where Hardy acknowledges the existence of some quirk or quality in human behaviour, his interest and sympathy are unfailingly engaged.

Hardy is not a resolver of differences. Poets like Yeats and Eliot delighted in wrestling with contraries, either to unite them, or at least to place them in a meaningful relationship. But Hardy lets the differences stand.

'Channel Firing' is a poem of long perspectives. 'And There was a Great Calm' is about a specific event: the signing of the Armistice. It is a poem about the hour that marked the difference between war and peace, and reading it would be an appropriate way to complete your work in this section.

6 GRIEF

6.1 Most of the poems we shall be looking at in this section were written in the years 1912–13. The section in the set book is called *Veteris vestigia flammae*, a quotation from Virgil which means something like 'ashes of an old fire'. (See the last poem in the sequence: 'Where the Picnic Was' p 68.)

Hardy's first wife, Emma, died in late November 1912. The marriage had begun in idyllic happiness, but it had ended in years of bitterness and hostile silence hidden behind a respectable public front which must have become increasingly difficult to maintain. They had first met in Cornwall, and in the spring following her death '... almost to a day, forty-three years after his first journey to Cornwall – he started for St Juliot, putting up at Boscastle, and visiting Pentargan Bay and Beeny Cliff, on which he had not once set foot in the long interval'. (*Life* p 361.) It was a kind of pilgrimage, and memory and grief combined to inspire some of the most moving poems he ever wrote.

Twenty-one poems were published together under the title *Veteris vestigia flammae*, and Creighton prints all of them (pp 49–68). The best are generally regarded as Hardy's finest poems, and if you feel that with a poet who wrote so much, you must concentrate on only a handful of pieces, it would be sensible to choose these. But I would caution any reader against the common assumption that this sequence contains the *only* good poems Hardy ever wrote. Read them through carefully before you read the critical discussion which follows.

6.2 Much of Hardy's poetry is difficult to talk about, but in this group the subject itself inhibits most readers still further: not just grief, but remorse and regret for a failed marriage. In the old-fashioned nursery phrase: it's rude to stare. Yet we have to remember that it is not only these poems of personal grief which discourage investigation. Hardy is habitually a kind of poetic recluse, who shows as much to the world as he has decided to permit, then slams the door against further snooping. So these poems of 1912–13 may not just seem quintessentially Hardy because they are especially *good*, but also because here the characteristic stance has met its perfect subject matter. Grief is a state of mind in which reticence is understandable, because it may be a kind of defence against renewed pain.

Grief, remorse, regret: it is difficult to say what these poems are about. They form a a clear group, yet each one is free-standing. One of their most moving themes is the sheer distance between the past happiness and present grief – the distance between Cornwall and the gloomy Victorian proprieties of Max Gate, their house near Dorchester; the distance represented by the forty-three years in which Cornwall went unvisited.

It seems proper that you should have a choice of opinions about these most-discussed of all Hardy's poems, and so I have arranged a selection of quotations from different critics, which you will find printed as Appendix 2. You can read both, or the appendix or this section alone: but whatever you do, do not skimp the time you spend on the poems.

6.3 I referred earlier to Hardy's awareness of the pains of hindsight (2.9). These poems are powerfully moving; but they are also indubitably strange. What are they? – Love poems to a dead woman? – Conversations with a ghost? They cannot be conveniently labelled, for they do not belong to any recognizable genre. Hardy had no pattern to follow, no poetic decorum. And so we should not bring to these poems any false expectations about what kind of style or diction might be appropriate to them. Nor, I think, can we refuse to take them seriously if we do not believe in ghosts: these ghosts are real because the poems make them so.

6.4 ■ In fact, the two matters are inseparable, for one of the questions this extraordinary group of poems should make us ask is: How, granted that one is a rational and not over-credulous being, does one address a ghost? Not a spook who has come to scare us, but a very special kind of 'familiar'.[9] It is a question so apparently foolish that few critics have dared to ask it: William Pritchard's article is particularly admirable because it does dare. I am not going to look at all twenty-one poems, but the first seems a good place to begin. Read 'The Going' and then read and make a careful assessment of one more comment from Pritchard:

> Imagine how one could ruin this [the last stanza] with a too-sprightly
> rendering of 'Well, well' or by attempting to read the assertions with a more
> slanted tone than they require. And what do they require? The answer to
> 'Why, then, latterly did we not speak', and to the imagining of
> might-have-been, must be such as to impress us with how literally
> unanswerable these matters are. Therefore ways of not answering must be
> relied upon: ellipsis, exclamation, the inexpressible toneless tone of 'Well,
> well!' In discussing this poem Douglas Brown speaks of 'a supremely *natural*
> use of the language of conversation and meditation, unassuming, pretending
> nothing'. Although I think I know what he means, I'd want to put more
> emphasis on what an odd kind of directness or naturalness it is that makes no
> concessions to the reader, doesn't try to ingratiate itself with him in any way,
> provides no clues for responding to the mutterings of 'It must go' or the blank
> space of an ellipsis. (Pritchard 'Hardy's anonymous sincerity'.)

Well, do you think you know what Brown means by 'a supremely *natural* use of the language of conversation and meditation'? And do you agree?

Discussion

It is a difficult question. There is nothing obscure about the diction. It makes use of colloquialisms, and many of its phrases would pass unnoticed in ordinary speech. What Brown means by 'meditation' I do not know: surely not the occupation of mystics? And how can we say what language is natural to simple thoughtfulness?

6.5 The poem opens with a direct commonplaceness that is startling. If Pritchard is right to ask what is the tone of voice of these poems then isn't it possible that the tone of the first line is something close to the horribly familiar 'line' (in a different sense):

[9] I mean the kind of attendant spirit that comes at a call. But most 'familiars' are traditionally supposed to be evil, and this is one neither specially evil nor good: only very human.

Why (on earth) didn't you tell me you were going out? Then I . . . etc. etc. I do not mean to be flippant. I am sure that this poem contains traces of a kind of conversation that is indeed supremely natural though not very admirable. Are there not several hints of blame, and the very language of a marriage gone sour as we know Hardy's had? A line such as 'Why do you make me leave the house . . . ' is of course very plaintive, but can a suggestion of blame and self-pity be entirely eliminated? Sadness is the dominant note as he asks the ghost why she forces him to recognize that she is not really there. But the undertones persist, and they are very chilling.

6.6 What is particularly remarkable about this poem (and indeed, many of Hardy's best) is its fluidity of tone. On each occasion where the characteristic tones of marital squabbling threaten there is an immediate modulation into something tenderer:

> Why did you give no hint that night
> That quickly after the *morrow's dawn*,
> And calmly, as if indifferent quite,
> You would close your term here, up and be gone
> > Where I could not follow
> > *With wing of swallow*
> *To gain one glimpse of you ever anon!*

I have italicized the phrases that check the faint bitterness. For what other reason would Hardy have included the line 'With wing of swallow' – merely for the rhyme? Surely for the tone: to snatch the stanza away from even the ghost of strife. Notice too how the word 'indifferent' suggests both a hint of callousness, and a curious kind of stateliness or dignity – as if her death were like the departure of a royal visitor.

6.7 In the second stanza the modulations are even more subtle. It begins with faint reproach, but the word 'lip' (which at first seems so odd) when followed by 'softest' suggests a kiss. 'Harden' too seems odd because it is fulfilling several functions, and no one in particular. It suggests the brightening light of the growing day; the sharper definition of the shadows; the approaching blow of her death; and I think (Hardy is not evasive, so why should his reader turn aside) it suggests what could not be said explicitly: that she died to spite him – her hardness persisted to the very end. And as long as she is hard, he is unmoved. But his state changes, when she, in dying, moves away beyond all change:

> . . . unknowing
> > That your *great going*
> *Had place* that moment, and altered all.

Again, the italicized phrases impart great dignity to her death. These phrases are generous: they imply a kind of forgiveness, despite the bitterness he cannot entirely forget. Indeed, one of the things the poem is about is not being able to forget. His loss is so painful because his memory is so vivid. But it is something like an act of defiance to include in his account of loss, hints of the very language of the rancour which he might have been expected *not* to regret losing.

6.8 Hardy calls this poem 'The Going'. He might have called it 'Her Death', or something of the sort, but the title he chose draws attention to a strange, mobile quality in the poem, a kind of melancholy wandering in thought, in and out of memory. Look at the way the poem moves in time.

The first two stanzas refer to the moment of death, the third to some time after her death – the time of writing. The passage of time is covered very smoothly: the first line of the third stanza echoes the form of the first line of the whole poem. But the third stanza ends with a terrifying 'perspective' of desolation. Then there is a dramatic change, and from the present and the worst, he moves back into the distant past 'While Life unrolled us its very best'. It is a glorious moment in the poem, but all it can achieve is a worsening of the pain in the two last stanzas.

6.9 In the second line of the fifth stanza Hardy uses the phrase 'those days long *dead*'. Of his wife's death, in the next line, he uses the word 'vanishing'. Nowhere in 'The Going' does he describe her as dead, though he describes himself as a dead man in the final stanza. The days are dead, and what 'We might have said' was never said. In the fifth stanza, though the tone is regretful, it is subdued. The anguish reasserts itself in the final stanza. The first line is conversational, almost. Perhaps the kind of words anyone might use to divert attention away from his grief. But notice how the second line changes. There is all the difference in the world between 'All's past amend' and 'It must go'. The second phrase might seem more vague, but surely its power lies in its horrifying, infinite inclusiveness? The last three and a half lines are in a weak sense a parallel with the lines in the same place in the previous stanza. Both stanzas seem to be about hindsight but what is different is more important than what is similar. Whereas in the first stanza he is thinking of what might have been, in the last he is lamenting what could never have been, because they did not try to rediscover the triumphal moments of their youth.∎

6.10 'The Going' is a journey she has taken without him; it is also a journey of another kind that they might have taken together. And it is also a more metaphysical kind of journey, in and out of possibility, until it ends face to face with the brutal fact. All the *Veteris vestigia flammae* poems form a carefully constructed sequence, and the notion of movement and travelling recurs continually.

6.11 In the first poem Emma is only beginning to be a ghost: her husband can address her, but only for a 'breath' is she the visible presence that appears more vividly in some of the later poems. Read the next three poems, 'Your Last Drive', 'The Walk' and 'Rain on a Grave'. The changes in his relationship with his dead wife are described step by step.

In the first three stanzas of 'Your Last Drive' there is again a somewhat strange combination of tones: sympathy with coldness. Another word might be aloofness, yet surely though Hardy is aware that he *was* aloof, that there was a tragic distance between them, the sympathy which has followed her death has narrowed the gap somewhat. There seem to be lingering traces of the bitterness and blame in stanza four, but these belong to the past, and the final stanza shows an awareness of their proper, their only possible place. This is not nearly such an exciting poem as 'The Going': its virtues are those of returning balance. In 'The Walk' the progression continues: all blame has disappeared, and been replaced by calm. It is none the less moving for that: indeed the intangibility of the criteria by which he measures his loss act as a kind of proof of emotion. As I said before, Hardy is often at his best when noticing the differences in things. 'Rain on a Grave' completes the first movement with its suggestions of possible harmony. But there has been no compromise.

6.12 There is no time for comment on all these poems, though I suggest that you pick one of those that go unmentioned, and write a brief commentary. But notice the progression of the sequence. Sympathy grows, though strangely, because Hardy has to put himself in a position of almost physical companionship with the dead. Eventually the sympathy is so intense that he can write a poem in the ghost's own voice: 'The Haunter'. Its simplicity is awesome. He imagines the answers he cannot hear; and they are the answers he wants to hear. 'The Haunter' is of course a fiction, whereas all the other poems seem a true record of his experience. And yet Hardy's clear need for this kind of answer gives this act of wish-fulfilment a right to a place in the sequence.

6.13 'The Voice' is probably the most famous poem in the sequence, and I have little to add to the comments quoted in Appendix 2. One thing needs saying: it is the saddest poem of the sequence. From this point on, although grief does not disappear, some strength is regained. 'The Voice' is the moment of greatest helplessness.

6.14 The title 'After a Journey' suggests rest, but in fact the poem is characterized by a nervous, slightly manic restlessness. The journey is a literal one – the pilgrimage to Cornwall that Hardy made six months after Emma's death. But instead of tranquillity, what succeeds is a kind of curious ghostly hide-and-seek. The poem is dazzling. It is immensely fast. It changes in mood and diction and pace continuously. Conventional haunting is a leisurely affair, but this is a chase, and its final note is surely exhaustion.   In its easy shift from tone to tone, this poem is worth comparing with 'The Going'. The formality of the opening lends a note of tragedy, but a transition to a very particularizing emotion is managed through the colloquial touches of the line 'Where you will next be there's no knowing'. The 'human' touch introduces the human presence – or her ghost; the colours have a human warmth about them which for the moment makes the visitation convincingly solid – though of course the phrase 'coming and going' is splendidly ambiguous.

The wistfulness disappears; for a moment it seems she is caught, and the second stanza combines triumph, confidence and challenge:

> What have you now found to say of our past –
>   Scanned across the dark space wherein I have lacked you?
> Summer gave us sweets, but autumn wrought division?
>   Things were not lastly as firstly well
>   With us twain, you tell?

But confidence evaporates in the following stanza, and the ghost retreats as the details of the real scene come crowding in. The end is surely terrifying:

> Trust me, I mind not, though Life lours,
>   The bringing me here; nay, bring me here again!
>   I am just the same as when
> Our days were a joy, and our paths through flowers.

But how can he be just the same? Perhaps he does not intend that his readers should believe he is. But he wants the ghost to believe it. The chase has been both exciting and tender, but as the poem reaches its end, it must travel through forty years to reach the present, and the final stanza begins on a note of weariness, even though it is dawn and not evening. The daylight hours are traditionally the resting-time of ghosts, and she is more tired than he is. The four final lines offer her love, and his arm to lean on. For her sake he will face even what has brought him to this place again: her death. And for her sake he will valiantly assert that he is 'just the same'. Perhaps he is implying that the difference between the man he was and the man he is, is far less important than that between the two of them: for he, though 'frail' (stanza 3 last line) is still alive.

6.15 You need not make up your mind at all, of course. Why should you when Hardy himself is so aware both of possibilities, and the impossibility of finding an answer to life's most urgent questions. 'Beeny Cliff' begins gloriously, and even the ominous cloud of the third stanza cannot obscure the poem's vigour. The momentum is such that we almost believe that the fourth stanza can be answered affirmatively; and something even survives into the last stanza – a kind of courage, or defiance. If I am right in suspecting the faintest trace of weariness in 'After a Journey' (a slight, defensive bowing of the head) then in contrast here the head is lifted, the jaw set. There is an impulse towards evasion, perhaps, in the euphemistic ' – elsewhere – ', but it is rejected with consummate bravery in the last line.

6.16 'After a Journey' is restless, excited and sad; 'Beeny Cliff' is heroic. 'At Castle Boterel' is more like an expression of faith. Donald Davie is right to stress that Hardy means what he says (see Appendix 2). It needs stressing, for what he says seems so irrational; but much of Hardy's work is characterized by a dogged determination to to say what he means. (And that even when his meaning includes the greatest ambiguities, as in some of the other pieces in this sequence.) For me, it is the greatest of Hardy's poems: not a word jars, and every moment convinces and moves me deeply. It is consciousness that I cannot do it justice, rather than any feeling that I might spoil it which makes me reluctant to say much about it. (Though I shall return to it in Part 2, Section 3.) What impresses me particularly is its plainness, and Hardy's authority over his material: neither quality seems particularly emotive. Yet how much is asserted without a trace of flamboyance. The style is exactly in keeping with the tremendous assertion that a simple, and apparently unremarkable moment was in truth the moment these rocks record. Not only the choice of words, but that famous clarity that Pound admired so much, and the sheer skill with which he sets ideas in their most articulate order, all combine to make this poem irrefutable. Even his consciousness of his own approaching death does not make him bate a word of his assertion that 'what they [the rocks] record in colour and cast/Is – that we two passed.'

6.17 A colleague comments 'The poem's greatness is that the memory will die with him. Hence the force of "shrinking".' But I would claim that the strenuous and daring positives in the poem are not threatened by the poet's approaching death, because the poem, and all that it asserts, survives. The individual dies, and his ghosts die with him. Hence the overpowering sadness of the last stanza. But the poem has given the moment a kind of immortality and something like the ghost of a ghost survives. When I ask myself, why did Hardy write these poems, the answer that seems most appropriate to me is emphatically *not* because he wanted his readers to know about his grief. Nor was he trying to lay a ghost. Far from it. Here as elsewhere, I believe his instinct was to record and preserve. These poems were written to keep alive what would otherwise have died with Thomas Hardy.

6.18 I want to end this section with something of an anticlimax. I suggested that these are the poems that you should probably concentrate on most, and you would do well to go back now and give those you have found most interesting another careful reading. But read 'Bereft' (p 210) and 'She Hears the Storm' (p 210). It may seem a little callous, but we need to be reminded that a grief that existed only in his imagination could also inspire in Hardy some exquisite poetry.

And before you begin re-reading your favourite poems in this sequence, read 'Under the Waterfall', the poem which originally preceded *Veteris vestigia flammae*. It is the real starting point for the poems of mourning. For 'Under the Waterfall' describes the days of happiness, with only the faintest premonition of the ghosts of bitterness which were to come.

THOMAS HARDY PART 2

Note The material contained in Part 2 Sections 1 and 2 may seem oddly placed, because it includes discussion of generalities of a sort usually found near the beginning of a conventional introduction. But many introductions make little sense, unless you know something of the work of the author concerned. There would, for example, be little point in worrying about Hardy's reputation amongst other critics and poets, if you yourself have no idea of what kind of reputation he might deserve. The first two sections also include references to later parts of this course, and to poets who are not included in this course at all. They have been designed for fairly quick reading: most of the work in this part is in the final section.

1 INTRODUCTION – HARDY'S REPUTATION

1.1 Thomas Hardy lived from 1840–1928. He was thus unquestionably a Victorian and, because his old age was vigorous, a man of the twentieth century too, still writing poetry when Pound, Eliot and Yeats were producing some of their greatest works. He is most famous as a novelist, and many of you will be familiar with his last and most controversial novel, *Jude the Obscure* (1896) which was included in the syllabus of A302 *The Ninteeenth-Century Novel and Its Legacy*.[1] Yet for the last thirty years of his life he abandoned the novels that had made him comfortably prosperous and devoted himself to his first and abiding but less remunerative love, poetry. He published a number of volumes of lyrics, amounting to nearly a thousand poems in all, though by his own account this was only a fraction of his output. Everyone who reads his collected poetry agrees that the work is extremely uneven in quality, and few, I suppose, can wish he had published more. But no one has ever managed to produce a definitive selection of Hardy's work. Apart from a comparatively small number of indubitably great poems, there is a vast middle area where no two people apparently think alike. This being the case, any anthology must be treated with reservations, and I have found it necessary to include in these units several poems not in your set book.

1.2 The dating of Hardy's poems is a mystery which, fortunately, need not worry us. He only supplied a few dates, the earliest ('Domicilium') 'between 1857 and 1860' and the latest, August 1927: a poetic career of about seventy years. It seems from the strangely impersonal biography which his second wife ghosted that he wrote some poetry practically every year between these dates and thus had a writing career longer than any other major English poet. Each published collection can tell us only the last possible date for the composition of the pieces it includes. Unless a date is given, there is no way of telling when a poem might have been written. For although each collection contains poems of greatly differing quality, it is generally agreed that Hardy, as a poet, did not 'develop'. There is no essential difference between the poems that we know to be early and the poems that we know to be late. There is no discernible progress, no sign that Hardy moved upwards and onwards on the shoulders of his past self. And there is very little evidence that he was influenced by the work or theory of contemporary poets.

[1] The Open University (1973) A302 *The Ninteeenth-century Novel and its Legacy*, Units 18–19 *Jude the Obscure*, The Open University Press.

1.3 So Hardy's contemporaneity with the 'modernist' poets does not give him an unquestionable right to be considered alongside them. But neither does he belong exclusively with the Victorians because of the date of his birth. By such standards Yeats (b. 1865) might also be called a Victorian. Was he then a loner, cut off from the past, present and future of English poetry? How can we 'place' the poetical achievement of Thomas Hardy?

1.4 ■ It will be useful to look at what various critics who have taken an overall view of the period of this course have to say about him. C. K. Stead, in *The New Poetic*, does not even mention him. Yet on the first page of his general introduction John Press says

> After the death of Swinburne in April 1909 and of Meredith in May,
> W. B. Yeats remarked 'And now I am King of the cats', forgetting perhaps
> that Thomas Hardy was still in the plenitude of his poetical genius. (Press
> *A Map of Modern English Verse* p 1.)

'forgetting perhaps' – does Press then forget it too? There is no separate chapter in his book on Hardy. A little later Press says emphatically 'While sharing this admiration [Larkin's] for Hardy I am convinced that the major poetic achievement of the century is the work of the modernist poets . . .' (p 4). Hardy, he implies, belongs 'to what one may call the alternative tradition'. I think you will find it useful to read from the last paragraph on p 4 of Press's book to the end of the chapter (p 5). Then look up Hardy in the index and make brief notes on the kind of references Press makes to him.

Discussion

1.5 I expect you will have noticed that in Press's estimate Hardy figures more as an 'influence' than as a poet in his own right – though, let it be said at once, the value of such a distinction is doubtful. On a possible relationship between Hardy and the 'modernist' poets who were at the height of their powers while he was still alive there is nothing. There are a couple of references to him in connection with the poetry of the First World War. But the majority of references (and they are not, all told, very many) concerns the admiration felt for him by three British poets of a later generation – Auden, Dylan Thomas and Larkin. And even here the nature of Hardy's influence is only vaguely assessed. On p 222, for example, Press can only say that 'Perhaps . . . Thomas was drawn towards Hardy by the attraction of opposites'. Of the relation between Hardy and Auden and Hardy and Larkin there will be more to say later: briefly and anticipatorily in these units, and more fully later in the units dealing with Auden and the poetry of the 1950s. But I suggest that you look carefully now at the quotations from Auden and Larkin on pp 190 and 259 respectively. Both of them cast doubts on any claims a critic might want to make for Hardy's modernism: Auden says 'He was modern without being too modern'. Larkin includes him amongst other poets not 'normally regarded as "modern" '. In an article published in 1966 Larkin asked 'Why doesn't Hardy attract more people who can write?' He was talking about the novels as well as the poetry, but I think there is a more serious shortage of good criticism of the poetry than of the novels. Larkin says

> Perhaps the oddest thing about contemporary Hardy criticism, however, is
> the way in which its mediocre perpetrators consider themselves justified
> in patronising Hardy's poems. . . . may I trumpet the assurance that one

reader at least would not wish Hardy's *Collected Poems* a single page shorter, and regards it as many times over the best body of poetic work this century so far has to show?

> . . . those whose names come to mind as the century's principal critics have really shown little interest in him. Eliot was hostile. Leavis patronising, Wilson, Empson, Blackmur, Trilling – none has been other than neglectful. (Larkin 'Wanted: Good Hardy Critic' *Critical Quarterly*.)

It would be foolish to pretend that this course can begin to correct the balance, though I can say that I have no intention of patronizing Thomas Hardy. Why has he been patronized? Did Henry James begin it when he called him 'the good little Thomas Hardy'? Words like naive, homespun, and rustic are all too common in attempts to define Hardy's characteristic tones. In a sense, Hardy's own Wessex may have rebounded on him, for too many people have insisted on seeing him as the immemorial yokel. Perhaps this has happened because as a poet he is so difficult to pin down: he does not unmistakably belong to a period or a style, and so in the popular and the critical imagination his name has become synonymous with a phoney rural scene (certainly not with his *real* Wessex) which is then supposed to account for everything about him. The question that is begged, of course, is why pin him down at all?■

1.6 ■ F. R. Leavis's *New Bearings in English Poetry* is a set book for another part of this course, but you may find it useful to look now at what he has to say about Hardy on pp 51–6. Is Larkin's complaint justified?

Discussion

There are things here which have never since been better expressed: 'that purity of recognition which is Hardy's strength. His verse has no incantation: it does what it says, and presents barely the fact recognized by a mind more than commonly responsible and awake'. (p 51.) Here, surely, Leavis has put his finger on the core of Hardy, and the very quality that sometimes makes him difficult to talk about: 'that purity of recognition' unerringly identifies what is important in a situation, and leaves the reader nothing to do except repeat the assertion. Talking about Hardy strains one's power of definition to the utmost.

But there are things in Leavis's brief account of Hardy which are not as acceptable:

> Hardy's solidity appears *archaic*
>
> Hardy is a *naive* poet of *simple attitudes and outlook*
>
> His originality was not of the kind that goes with a *high degree of critical awareness*: it went, indeed, with a *naive* conservatism.

The italics are mine, of course. What does 'critical' mean in that last quotation? Many readers, I suspect, have taken it to mean that Hardy was deficient in good literary taste.

Maybe you should reserve judgement on these opinions until you have studied more of Hardy's poetry. Certainly these are not of course entirely unfounded remarks. But there are two major assumptions which I think must be questioned. The first is that Hardy was a Victorian, and therefore out of date and out of touch long before 1932 – the date of *New Bearings*. At that time Leavis could not foresee that

Hardy's influence might skip a generation.[2] Secondly, Leavis must be held responsible for the opinion which achieved almost mythic status amongst critics, that Hardy wrote only a handful of good poems: 'his rank as a major poet rests upon a dozen poems'. As we have already seen, Larkin challenges this view. But it is not so much Leavis's claim that there are only a dozen good pieces that is dangerous, as the grounds on which he distinguishes the good from the bad.

> These [the good few] are lost among a vast bulk of verse interesting only by its oddity and idiosyncrasy, and as illustrating the habits that somehow become strength in his great poetry.

Do you think that crucial 'somehow' is fully explained in what follows? The word 'lost' also needs looking at carefully.■

1.7   Much more could be said about these very packed pages, but my purpose is to give you some idea of Hardy's reputation among major poets and critics. Compared with Eliot, Hardy must appear, as Leavis said 'A naive poet of simple attitudes and outlook', and it was in Eliot, and in Pound and Yeats, that Leavis believed the future strength of poetry was to be found. Eliot himself disliked Hardy's novels, and virtually ignored his poetry.

1.8   Ezra Pound's assessment was more favourable, and surely more just. I have already quoted his remark: 'Now *there* is a clarity. There is the harvest of having written twenty novels first.'

Pound admired Hardy, and wanted to include some of his poetry in an anthology he was helping to publish. But his evaluation included a clear consciousness of Hardy's difference – ' . . . he woke one to the extent of his own absorption in *subject* as contrasted with aesthetic preoccupation with "treatment".' (Letters 205.) However, like many subsequent critics, Pound felt there was much amiss with Hardy's poetry, even if ultimately what was wrong was less important than the 'solid centre'. ' . . . it is only maturer patience that can sweep aside a writer's honest error, and overlook unaccomplished clumsiness or outlandishness or old fashionedness, for the sake of the solid centre'. (Pound *The ABC of Reading* p 193.)

1.9   Pound was consistently more generous towards his contemporaries than Eliot: he was much more tolerant, for example, of the Georgian poets in their early years. And it may be the existence of the Georgian poets which does much to account for Hardy's reputation. I think he was tacitly numbered amongst them, and consequently not taken very seriously. You will remember from Unit 1 *English Poetry in 1912* what an amorphous group they were; it would be easy to assume that a poet like Hardy who did not fit in smoothly elsewhere was a kind of Georgian fellow-traveller. Are there not phrases in Edmund Blunden's 'The Waggoner' (quoted in Unit 1, 4.21) that remind you of Hardy?

2   HARDY AND TRADITION

2.1   As we have prepared this course, one of the problems we have been most acutely aware of is the obvious and inescapable one that the poetry of this period, like every

---

[2]Generations among poets are difficult to date. Auden was already writing some of his most Hardy-like poetry in the 'Twenties.

living thing and everything made by men, has its ancestry and its traditions. Everything is the product of the past, of a peculiar combination of anterior circumstances. The qualities of twentieth-century poetry have been partially determined by contemporary pressures, but those pressures are themselves produced by the continuing processes of history of which the poetry is itself a part. The strong reactions which made the poetry of Pound and Eliot so new were reactions against what had happened in the past: any revolutionary (whether poet or politician) understands that what is wrong in the present, and what needs to be changed, is the result of things that have happened in the past. This is obvious, and some of the applications of this general truth (or truism) to the particular problems of the poet in the early twentieth-century were discussed in Unit 1.

Few things, perhaps none, are ever as new as they seem. This is something which every researcher into any aspect of humanitarian studies must face up to sooner or later. To realize this is both baffling and pleasing. As soon as you look more closely at what appears to be a new development you realize that the plant has sprung from a very complex and far-reaching system of roots, and that probably you never will find the true starting point. All sorts of analogies with weeding an overgrown garden suggest themselves, but none of them are apt, because the pleasures of discovering and following these fine strands are the opposite of the frustrations involved in trying to rid your patch of bindweed.

2.2 These remarks may seem to be irrelevant, but I mean them first to stand as a kind of apology, or at least to introduce an acknowledgement of some of the anomalies that this free standing course on twentieth-century poetry commits us to. Behind the poetry of this period is the literature of many centuries: the literature too of many different cultures and languages. We cannot and do not ask that you should know anything about these antecedent literatures. You may feel more comfortable if you know something, but whether it is actually necessary is arguable. In designing the course, we have tried to minimize the problem, but we cannot ignore it, for the simple reason that the poets we shall be studying were intensely aware of the traditions from which they sprang, and often acknowledged their indebtedness quite openly in their poetry. Yet at the same time what from the past was no longer vital had to be rejected. T. S. Eliot's essay 'Tradition and the Individual Talent' (reprinted in the Course Reader) puts forward a view that is not so much an answer as a way of living with a perpetual dilemma. We insist, says Eliot

> when we praise a poet, upon the aspects of his work in which he least
> resembles anyone else. In these aspects of parts of his work we pretend to
> find what is individual, what is the peculiar essence of the man. We dwell
> with satisfaction upon the poet's difference from his predecessors; we
> endeavour to find something that can be isolated in order to be enjoyed.
> Whereas if we approach a poet without this prejudice we shall often find
> that not only the best, but the most individual parts of his work may be
> those in which the dead poets, his ancestors, assert their immortality most
> vigorously.

As in much, if not all, his criticism, Eliot is here trying to define a firm, objective basis for his own experience. He, and men like him (sympathetic contemporary poets) have praised the new at the expense of the old; they have happily cut themselves away from their immediate past, and now Eliot begins to ask what has been lost in the severance. How can a poet be fully of the present and yet make best use of the past that went to making that present?

2.3 In the second part of this essay, Eliot examines the importance of the poet's personality to his work, and concludes that the best art is that in which there is least of the poet's individual character and emotional experience:

the more perfect the artist, the more completely separate in him will be
the man who suffers and the mind which creates; the more perfectly will
the mind digest and transmute the passions which are its material.

Indeed, Eliot claimed that the artist had no need to experience or to suffer what he wrote about. What he is deploring is the extreme Romantic stance, the poet whose single subject is his own response to the world. It is a prohibition which seems to include Hardy, many of whose greatest poems record the events and emotions of his own life. In the following passage, notice how Hardy might be considered admirable according to some of Eliot's criteria, and excluded by others:

> The business of the poet is not to find new emotions, but to use the
> ordinary ones and, in working them up into poetry, to express feelings
> which are not in actual emotions at all. And emotions which he has never
> experienced will serve his turn as well as those familiar to him. Consequently,
> we must believe that 'emotion recollected in tranquillity' is an inexact
> formula. For it is neither emotion, nor recollection, nor, without distortion
> of meaning, tranquillity. It is a concentration, and a new thing resulting
> from a concentration, of a very great number of experiences which to the
> practical and active person would not seem to be experiences at all; it is a
> concentration which does not happen consciously or of deliberation. These
> experiences are not 'recollected', and they finally unite in an atmosphere
> which is 'tranquil' only in that it is a passive attending upon the event. Of
> course this is not quite the whole story. There is a great deal, in the writing
> of poetry, which must be conscious and deliberate. In fact, the bad poet is
> usually unconscious where he ought to be conscious, and conscious where
> he ought to be unconscious. Both errors tend to make him 'personal'. Poetry
> is not a turning loose of emotion, but an escape from emotion; it is not the
> expression of personality, but an escape from personality.

2.4　Eliot quotes Wordsworth's phrase 'emotion recollected in tranquillity' because it is one of the most famous definitions of poetry to be used by a Romantic poet and because Wordsworth proudly, though not self-indulgently, wrote about his own personality in a way that was obnoxious to Eliot. But why turn all his fire against a poet so long dead? The answer must be that Eliot's notion of what Wordsworth had been was obscured by the later and often degenerate growths of Romanticism which would have appalled the early Wordsworth as much as they appalled Eliot. This is not the place to discuss unlikely-sounding similarities between Wordsworth and Eliot but it is certainly fair to say that like all great poets who have advanced their chosen art, both were early impelled by an intense desire to be clear of the hampering, worn-out modes which were all that their immediate predecessors seemed to have bequeathed them. T. S. Eliot may not have recognized this likeness, but I want later to suggest that Thomas Hardy did, and that Wordsworth was an important influence on his work.

2.5　Even the greatest criticism cannot last like poetry. We do not read Sidney's, or Johnson's, or Coleridge's or Matthew Arnold's criticism for its everlasting truths, but because it tells us by what standards the best critical intelligences of their generation made their judgements. 'Tradition and the Individual Talent', is now as much a period piece as Arnold's *Culture and Anarchy*. (Though of course both contain ideas still worthy of the most careful scrutiny.) Eliot's essay is particularly interesting because it helps to define the preoccupation of this whole generation of poets. Eliot was not the only one who wanted to cast off the baleful influences of the immediate past, yet felt a desperate need of roots in some poetic tradition. Pound and Yeats were also repelled by the exaggerated place of personality, and perhaps worse, of opinion, in the poetry of the late nineteenth and early twentieth century. All three chose to write impersonally, as if from hearts and minds that might not be their own.

2.6 We have already seen how difficult it is to talk about the personality of Hardy, and how it enters his poetry. He writes out of his own experience, but with a meticulous reticence that prevents the reader from getting too close to him. Perhaps this is his equivalent of the Yeatsian mask, or Eliot's assumed personae. On the other hand, his style is idiosyncratic to an extraordinary degree. He uses a variety and a complexity of metre greater than any other English poet before him. Less successfully, he seems to have imagined that the language was still as flexible as it was in the time of Shakespeare, and his habits of coining words, or using them in unorthodox ways frequently give his poetry a tinge of perverse awkwardness. Samuel Hynes, a critic who finds Hardy interesting and in many ways admirable, claims that his constant experiments indicate a failure to find a form which would suit what he had to say. This failure

> was surely due more to the disintegration of tradition which took place during his life, a process which he felt acutely as an Englishman and as a a poet. Like other poets of his time, Hardy was left without a poetic vehicle adequate to his needs. He spent his life trying to build another out of old parts, and his *Collected Poems* is a scrapyard of ideas that did not work. That it also contains some great, living poems is testimony to the power of his peculiar poetic gifts to transcend what seem impossible obstacles, and to make poetry out of the ill-assorted materials that were all he had. (Hynes *The Pattern of Hardy's Poetry* p 88.)

You will have a fair idea of what those ill-assorted materials were from Unit 1.

2.7 Creighton has collected most of Hardy's recorded observations about his poetic theory in his two appendices (Creighton, pp 307–28). They can be read very quickly.

The first three short Prefaces (to *Wessex Poems, Poems of the Past and Present,* and *Time's Laughingstocks and Other Verses*) all contain very similar assertions:

> The pieces are in a large degree dramatic or personative in conception; and this even where they are not obviously so. (1898)

> Of the subject-matter of this volume – even that which is in other than narrative form – much is dramatic or impersonative even where not explicitly so. (1901)

> . . . the sense of disconnection, particularly in respect of those lyrics penned in the first person, will be immaterial when it is borne in mind that they are to be regarded, in the main, as dramatic monologues by different characters. (1909)

Wessex Poems includes 'Hap'; 'Neutral Tones'; 'Thoughts of Phena'; 'To a Motherless Child'; 'Nature's Questioning'; 'At an Inn' and ' "I looked into my glass" ', as well as many ballads. *Poems of the Past and Present* includes poems on the Boer War and about Italy (cf. Creighton pp 101–6) 'A Commonplace Day'; 'At a Lunar Eclipse'; 'The Subalterns'; 'To an Unborn Pauper Child'; 'To Lizbie Brown'; 'A Broken Appointment'; 'A Wasted Illness'; 'The Self-Unseeing'; and 'In Tenebris'. *Time's Laughingstocks* includes 'The House of Hospitalities'; 'A Church Romance'; 'The Roman Road'; 'After the Last Breath'; 'One we Knew'.

2.8 It is worth looking at *a few* of the poems from this list, and trying to decide for what purpose Hardy made the disclaimers in his Prefaces. There are indeed many poems, like the ballads, which are unmistakably dramatic monologues. But why does he apparently want to dissuade his readers from thinking that the other first person narratives record his own experiences and views? Is it a rather naive attempt to preserve his privacy? Or is it after all true? Should we read many of the apparently personal poems as if they were fictions? In either case can we not see here an impulse related to Eliot's attack on the personal element in contemporary poetry? All his readers assume that some of Hardy's finest poems are indeed records of his personal grief. But what he says in his Prefaces indicates a conviction that personality, or truth to his own life, was not and should not be the quality which made them valuable.

2.9 Eliot, as I said earlier (Part 2, 1.7) was no admirer of Hardy. Even if they do share a preference for the notion of impersonality, and occupy some common ground in their mutual anxieties about how to reconcile the traditions of the past with the needs of the present, what divides them is more obvious and more important.

2.10 They are divided by Hardy's Victorian allegiances. Of these, the foremost influence on Hardy was Wordsworth, the founder of the Romantic, 'personal' school of poetry in English. At least, that is what the Victorians made of him – and indeed, it was what the later Wordsworth made of himself. But Hardy is responsive only to certain aspects of Wordsworth.

2.11 The first of these is the earlier poet's theories about the language proper to poetry. Wordsworth was disgusted by the over-elaborate, worn-out and artificial diction which the contemporary poets of his youth felt was necessary to lift poetry above the commonplace. He advocated instead a return to something nearer the 'real language of men'[3] and demonstrated his beliefs in two volumes of poetry, the *Lyrical Ballads* of 1798 and 1800. Their title indicates something of the nature of their language, and also suggests a possible reason why they might appeal to Hardy: the ballads again – a shadowy common presence. Perhaps the famous 'Lucy' poems (first printed in *Lyrical Ballads*) are closest to Hardy. Compare the following poem with Hardy's 'The Walk', and 'Rain on a Grave'.

> She dwelt among th'untrodden ways
>   Beside the springs of Dove,
> A maid whom there were none to praise
>   And very few to love.
>
> A violet by a mossy stone
>   Half-hidden from the Eye!
> Fair, as a star when only one
>   Is shining in the sky!
>
> She *liv'd* unknown, and few could know
>   When Lucy ceased to be;
> But she is in her Grave, and Oh!
>   The difference to me.

2.12 Both poets wrote their finest poetry out of personal memory. Wordsworth believed that it was the quality of his childhood which had made him a poet, and his efforts to recapture that time, in *The Prelude* and elsewhere do indeed confirm that in his early life were the sources of his power. In Hardy, the importance of memory seems to have been almost accidental, and for the most part, what is remembered is not childhood, but young manhood, and the happy exhilarating days of courtship. Nor does he recall the past as the very process by which poetry is made; he recalls it for comparison with an embittered, lonely present.

[3]Preface to *Lyrical Ballads* 1800.

Yet there are some of Hardy's poems which remind the reader of Wordsworth very powerfully, because they echo the Wordsworthian belief that the quality of a person's maturity depends on childhood experience. Read 'Childhood Among the Ferns' (p 93).

So many of Hardy's poems begin well and end lamely. So often, as long as the poem is purely narrative or descriptive we are happy, even mildly excited by the effortless skill with which the thing is done. But, as here, the interpretative, moralizing turn brings a sinking of the heart:

> Why should I have to grow to man's estate,
> And this afar-noised World perambulate?

It is not the thought that offends, but the diction; and that not simply because it is so awkward, but because it is so grotesquely adult. The rest of the poem has succeeded because it has kept to the scale of the fern-roofed den. On the whole we are convinced that these are a child's perceptions. Like Dickens at the beginning of *Great Expectations* Hardy realizes the importance of the simple fact that the child is *smaller* than the man. A child might think, I wish I could stay here forever; but only a goblin would think what Hardy says he thought.

However, I am less concerned with the faults of this poem than with its central Wordsworthian belief in the values of the child's perceptions. This is a poem that could only have been written by someone who admired not just Wordsworth's style, but his thought. At first, it seems to be simply a description of something any country-raised child with a taste for solitude might do. But notice how carefully insistent are the suggestions of shelter and solace. And it is the sweet breath from the ferns, restored by the sun, which quite literally inspires the thought 'I could live on here thus till death'. This thought occurs despite the discomfort he can only pretend not to notice. We have already observed Hardy's emphasis on the value that may lie in the most commonplace incident. This too is a belief he shared with, and may have derived from, Wordsworth. In the earlier poet the most splendid instances of recognizing the innate richness in moments a lesser sensibility may not notice, concern the common pursuits of childhood.

2.13   So Hardy's loyalty to Wordsworth made him by the standards of the early twentieth century a Victorian, and therefore beyond the pale. But Eliot certainly was looking at Hardy in a distorted perspective. He failed to recognize that Hardy's choice of allegiances, to the timeless ballad tradition, and a poet born in the eighteenth century, did not make him one with the minor poets who had simply and un-adventurously followed their immediate predecessors. Nor did the 'modernist' critics fully realize that the Wordsworth they despised was Wordsworth seen through Matthew Arnold's schoolmasterly Victorian eyes. They underestimated Hardy's independence. His originality was not theirs, but they were wrong to despise it. Samuel Hynes says: 'Hardy died as a poet, as he died as a man, without heirs'. (Hynes *The Pattern of Hardy's Poetry* p 73.) And at the time of Hardy's death, despite Pound's admiration, this would indeed have seemed the case. But after a generation, Hardy's influence revived again, in the poetry of Auden and Larkin. Curiously there is another parallel with Wordsworth here: *his* immediate successors (Byron, Shelley and even Keats) thought him dull and old-fashioned. But his influence revived again in mid-century, perhaps finding a purer, finer expression in the novels of George Eliot than in the poetry of Matthew Arnold.

2.14   Let me sum up rather crudely. Hynes says Hardy had no heirs. In fact, we know his grandsons, but not his sons. And in Wordsworth we can recognize his poetic grandfather; in the ballads his distant ancestry and his cousins – but, poetically speaking, who was Hardy's father?

You may object, that this is a question we need not ask, and that all the bother about influences is just something critics do to keep themselves warm in winter. But there are two answers to this, and the most interesting is the least relevant here. First of all, there is nothing new under the sun; all matter is matter recreated; all thoughts only variations on old thoughts. Of course this is a wicked generalization, but it is the more humane, and the more realistic course to ask what antecedent causes produced a poet's peculiar combination of ideas, than to imagine him as a man in total isolation from the minds, and even the company of his fellows. Second, in Hardy's case, there is a more local need – the dilemma expressed by T. S. Eliot, and shared by all the important poets of his generation, among whom I would number Hardy, though Eliot himself might not.

POSTSCRIPT

2.15   Of course it will be much easier to judge the influence of Hardy on a later generation of British poets when you reach the point of studying them in the course. But, to anticipate briefly read the following poem by W. H. Auden, and try to decide whether anything in it reminds you of Hardy.

Their Lonely Betters

As I listened from a beach-chair in the shade
To all the noises that my garden made,
It seemed to me only proper that words
Should be withheld from vegetables and birds.

A robin with no Christian name ran through
The Robin-Anthem which was all it knew,
And rustling flowers for some third party waited
To say which pairs, if any, should get mated.

No one of them was capable of lying,
There was not one which knew that it was dying
Or could have with a rhythm or a rhyme
Assumed responsibility for time.

Let them leave language to their lonely betters
Who count some days and long for certain letters;
We, too, make noises when we laugh or weep,
Words are for those with promises to keep.

Now read the following poem by Philip Larkin.

Sad Steps

Groping back to bed after a piss
I part thick curtains, and am startled by
The rapid clouds, the moon's cleanliness.

Four o'clock: wedge-shadowed gardens lie
Under a cavernous, a wind-picked sky.
There's something laughable about this,

The way the moon dashes through clouds that blow
Loosely as cannon-smoke to stand apart
(Stone-coloured light sharpening the roofs below)

High and preposterous and separate –
Lozenge of love! Medallion of art!
O wolves of memory! Immensements! No,

One shivers slightly, looking up there.
The hardness and the brightness and the plain
Far-reaching singleness of that wide stare

Is a reminder of the strength and pain
Of being young; that it can't come again,
But is for others undiminished somewhere.

Instead of a general comparison, read Hardy's poems 'I look into my glass' (p 109) and 'Shut out that Moon' (p 122) which have a related theme. In both cases (Auden's and Larkin's) you will want to compare attitudes as well as diction. Which do you think the more important – a similarity of style and attitude, or a similarity of diction? This is a question you may want to return to at the end of these units.

And in anticipation of some closer work (in Units 4–5) you might like to read 'Snow in the Suburbs' (p 11) which Donald Davie says is an Imagist poem:

> . . . Imagism . . . is concerned with *equations* for emotional experience, not presentation of it through images, still less implications or evocations of attendant physical properties. (Davie *Thomas Hardy and British Poetry* p 47.)

3 HARDY'S RELATIVISM – ANOTHER ATTEMPT TO PLACE HIM IN HIS TIMES

3.1 So far, what evidence we have discovered of Hardy's attitude to the society he lived in has suggested only a mild and rather private protest. We saw how divided he could be when we looked at his war poetry. Now I want to look at how much of a Victorian he was – how far he accepted Victorian values in taste and morals. Throughout these units I have pressed my view that Leavis was wrong to call Hardy a Victorian poet. But a man born in 1840 has to be a Victorian in some sense.

3.2 His poetic style is hardly typical of any period but the subject matter of many of his lesser poems captures the flavour of Victorian life as no one else has done.

Read 'A Nightmare, and the Next Thing' (p 136), 'Her Dilemma' (p 193), 'The Convergence of the Twain' (p 216), 'In the Study' (p 220), 'Midnight on the Great Western' (p 228). (There is no need to make notes on all of them, but read each carefully, and mark any passages that strike you in any way.)

I do not know whether Hardy invented the phrase 'A type of decayed gentility' ('In the Study'), but the whole poem, unprofound though it may be, strikes the reader as a very authentic observation. This is one of the relatively infrequent occasions when I find myself remembering the novelist in Hardy, who considers it worth noticing that the lady is 'almost breakfastless', and who catches so well

her polite reluctance to suggest that she needs money. This piece shares with 'Her Dilemma' a sense that it is part of a much longer story. It is like nothing so much as those Victorian paintings where a complex narrative is conveyed in a single frozen moment: the Church reminding her of her duty to tell the truth; her lover's wasted face of her equal duty to comfort the sick.

3.3 The other three poems in this random group are more interesting, because each contains a kind of questioning. 'A Nightmare and the Next Thing' seems to have been a very late poem: perhaps the next thing is death. Not only the 'six laughing mouths' on their way to a dance are gay; so are the 'three clammy casuals' on their way to the workhouse. But for the narrator, the scene is a nightmare. He gives no reason, only suggests that he is suffering from a kind of isolation.

> The house-fronts all seem backwise turned
> As if the outer world were spurned . . .

The misery on a festival day, the fog ('lamps . . . like dandelion-globes in the gloom') and the rejection, where even the poorest find some happiness – these are Dickensian themes. And like the older novelist, Hardy discovered a great imaginative stimulus in the railway. (He was old enough to recall the days when it had been new to Dorset, and it always retained the Victorian flavour of being a new thing in his poetry: it seems odd to find him mentioning a car – see 'Nobody Comes', p 135.) In 'Midnight on the Great Western' it is not a story which attracts him, but an enigma, and the possibility of a story – why is the boy travelling so late and alone? Here the Wordsworthian impulse to celebrate the qualities of childhood coincides with the unfortunate but characteristic decline in the last stanza which the poem does not need: it creaks with its efforts to be lofty, and achieves only a hollow sentimentality. But the rest of the poem is splendid, particularly in its combination of specific, descriptive detail and symbolic suggestion:

> . . . and a string
> Around his neck bore the key of his box,
> That twinkled gleams of the lamps' sad beams
> Like a living thing.

3.4 That Victorian fascination with the technology of the new transport makes a part of the most famous poem in this group, 'The Convergence of the Twain', which commemorates the sinking of the 'unsinkable' *Titanic* on her maiden voyage in 1912. Indeed, the launching of the *Titanic* was perhaps the last time a general and unsceptical optimism and self-congratulation greeted technological advance. Her loss was not just a tragedy (fifteen hundred people were drowned): it was seen by many – not just the superstitious – as a portent. A deck-hand is supposed to have told an embarking passenger that 'God himself could not sink this ship' and many people saw in the sinking a Divine warning that man would do well not to get above himself – even Hardy, who did not believe in God, and had to substitute the Immanent Will (i.e. the Will permanently pervading the Universe). The *Titanic* disaster was another of the events which made the year 1912 so oddly significant – perhaps the true end of the Victorian era.

3.5 Hardy's poem was not composed spontaneously. Another of its Victorian features is that it was written for the 'Dramatic and Operatic Matinee in Aid of the "Titanic" Disaster Fund'. Yet it is an impressive piece. Its vocabulary is particularly striking. We are used to a mixture of complex words and even difficult coinages with the vocabulary of plain speech in Hardy's poetry, but here the 'difficult' words predominate. Yet as always what strikes us is the deliberation with which they have been chosen. And here the effect is very special: it brings into the poem a note of chilly calculation that is finally terrifying:

> Alien they seemed to be:
> No mortal eye could see
> The intimate welding of their later history,
>
> Or sign that they were bent
> By paths coincident
> On being anon twin halves of one august event.

This note is appropriate to both halves of the august event, for not only does it give conviction to the notion of the Immanent Will (which might otherwise be hard to take); it also underlines the combination of human characteristics that went to the making of the *Titanic* – intellect and wilfulness. Notice how particularly appropriate is the word 'welding' in the ninth stanza.

3.6 Hardy wrote two novels which many of his first readers (including his wife) found deeply shocking: *Tess of the D'Urbervilles* and *Jude the Obscure*. Both challenged current proprieties about sex and religion. And although the *Collected Poems* contains many pieces with a very Victorian flavour (proportionally far more than Creighton includes, for not all are among the best) there are also many written in a spirit of reaction to conventional standards of belief and behaviour. Some merely cock a snook; others are a more serious attack. Read as many as you have time for from the following list: 'The Ruined Maid' (p 193); 'A Beauty's Soliloquy during her Honeymoon' (p 195); 'The Respectable Burgher' (p 199); 'The Curate's Kindness' (p 200); 'In the Cemetery' (p 220); 'Over the Coffin' (p 221); 'A Hurried Meeting' (p 250); 'An Evening in Galilee' (p 253); 'A Practical Woman' (p 255); 'Her Second Husband Hears her Story' (p 256).

3.7 Again, a very mixed bunch as far as their success goes. 'The Ruined Maid' is the most famous, and surely deserves to be as the funniest of all Hardy's intentionally comic poems. The novelist, the delighter in the details of life, the lover of 'life's little ironies' all combine here. The situation is a commonplace of fiction, but with the moral element omitted – or reversed. This ruined maid has done very nicely, and is *not* apparently heading for disease, remorse, and a lonely, early, grave. Her virtuous sister has the worst of the bargain. But the joke would be nothing if it were not for the witty economy of the dialogue. 'Some polish is gained with one's ruin', said she. 'Ruined' of course was a standard euphemism with a very definite meaning. But because to the uninitiated it is ambiguous (a vital part in the use of euphemism) Hardy can reconstruct another meaning for the word, which is quite the opposite of the conventional usage.

3.8 Hardy delighted in turning all kinds of assumptions on their heads. 'A Curate's Kindness' was prompted by a desire to take a fresh look at an assumption made by the liberal humanitarians from Wordsworth, through Dickens and beyond – namely that there was no charity in the workhouse. It is of a piece with Hardy's liking for the odd, for the incident that would not normally be noticed, that he likes to show that every rule can be disproved by an exception. Reading through Hardy's *Collected Works* one is sometimes reminded of the *New Statesman's* 'This England' column: these poetic scraps, which Hardy insists are the real world, are much more peculiar than fiction.

3.9 There is no need for further comment on Hardy's sardonic pieces about sex and marriage: everyone knows (or thinks he knows) about Victorian inhibitions – it's a knowledge that is part of the excitement of freedom. The Victorian attitude to death is almost equally a part of everyone's general knowledge, and so we can guess at the shocked response to a couplet like this:

> But all their children were laid therein
> At different times, like sprats in a tin.

('In the Cemetery')

It *is* shocking. In many of these poems Hardy intended not to be mildly ironic, but to be brutal. If you have not already done so, read 'An Evening in Galilee' (p 253).

And yet of course such naturalism about the New Testament was an attitude shared by many intellectuals. The pre-Raphaelite painters were attacked for the 'realism' of their religious paintings. Briefly, this is the 'higher criticism' that the Respectable Burgher finds so disturbing. (See Creighton p 199.) Hardy's atheism was as much a reaction as an intellectual conviction, but it was a reaction which he shared with many of his contemporaries.

3.10   We have already seen that Hardy's atheism does not preclude for him a kind of afterlife: his poetry is crowded with ghosts. Nor does his atheism preclude a kind of God: the most famous being the Immanent Will of 'The Convergence of the Twain'. Hardy believed to the point of obsession that life has pattern, even if it has no meaning.

Hardy's philosophical and religious poetry is frequently ignored; largely, I suspect because his readers are nervous of the task it seems to imply: the extracting of a consistent theory from a diverse mass of poetry. In fact, this is not only unnecessary, but Hardy himself prohibited it. In the notes at the back of your anthology, Creighton has written an excellent short essay, introducing the section he has called *Belief and Unbelief*. There he shows how Hardy frequently denied he had any consistent philosophy: his poems were 'impressions', ideas of the moment which were never seen by him as part of a coherent structure. Creighton admirably demonstrates how in Hardy's childhood the faith of his community established in him emotional needs which later in life were constantly challenged by intellectual speculation. His naive faith had no satisfactory answer to these attacks, but nothing could replace it, and he continued to wish he could still believe: 'The Oxen' (p 91) is the most famous expression of this dilemma.

> The poems in this section then should not be read as philosophic or didactic. They record subjectively the lifelong dialogue between Hardy's simple but unalienable Christian sentiments, his rational rejection of them, his wholly individual sense of the numinous in nature. A superficial reading may find them monotonous, indigestible, stultified and stultifying – Hardy at his most gristly as it has been, I think misguidedly, put to me. Closer inspection will reveal their startling variety and inconsistency, their wide range of poetic tone and register, and their extraordinary imaginative power. (Creighton p 343.)

Read the whole of Creighton's short essay, and as many of the poems in the section *Belief and Unbelief* as you have time for. If you have to make a choice, I would suggest 'Hap' (p 141); 'Nature's Questioning' (p 147); 'The Subalterns' (p 148); 'New Year's Eve' (p 157); 'God's Education' (p 158); 'A Plaint to Man' (p 159).

3.11   Creighton is absolutely right to insist that we should not try to find a system in Hardy's philosophy. Try to do so, and you will find yourself thinking that Hardy was rather a stupid man, over-impressed by the random juxtapositions of life, and trying to build a philosophy out of irony. But look at each poem distinctly, and you will be impressed by Hardy's intelligence, and his extraordinary alertness to anomalies.

3.12 In 'A Plaint to Man', God reproaches man for having invented him: man would have been better off without God. The poem is the mirror opposite of those where God regrets having created man. It is, of course, a logical absurdity, as Hardy knows perfectly well. I do not know whether the analogy is generally helpful, but in this kind of poem Hardy reminds me of science fiction writers; he projects from what we know – or what we generally accept, which comes to the same thing – out into the speculative dimensions. The resulting liberation is strangely invigorating. We have had reason before to notice how Hardy faces up to things: in many of these poems his stance becomes daring, a kind of courage:

> And now that I dwindle day by day
> Beneath the deicide eyes of seers
> In a light that will not let me stay,
>
> And tomorrow the whole of me disappears,
> The truth should be told, and the fact be faced
> That had best been faced in earlier years:
>
> The fact of life with dependence placed
> On the human heart's resource alone,
> In brotherhood bonded close and graced
>
> With loving-kindness fully blown,
> And visioned help unsought, unknown.

3.13 In the extract from 'Hardy's anonymous sincerity' quoted in the Course Reader, William Pritchard talks about the difficulty of recognizing Hardy's tone. Yet curiously, once you have accepted that a god who is merely an invention should have enough independence to reprove his creator, then you feel an absurd confidence that this is just how such a god might talk. Those critics who find themselves especially put out by Hardy's quirks of language have objected that his diction is at its oddest in these poems: 'Hap' is frequently quoted simply to show how peculiar Hardy's expression can be:

> How arrives it joy lies slain,
> And why unblooms the best hope ever sown?
> – Crass Casualty obstructs the sun and rain,
> And dicing Time for gladness casts a moan . . . .
> These purblind Doomsters had as readily strown
> Blisses about my pilgrimage as pain.

We have already discussed Hardy's diction in earlier sections, especially in connection with the memorial love poems of 1912–13. I want to suggest that it is much more acceptable in these poems of *Belief and Unbelief* than it is in the love poetry. Hardy's style is not necessarily wrong there – you will already have made up your mind about what you can tolerate. But it is easier to accept in poetry that is more obviously philosophical and intellectual, and less emotional than the poems to his dead wife. Of course, the memorial poems are decidedly *not* unintellectual: they are often unblinkingly analytical – a feature which paradoxically adds to their emotional power. Nor are poems like 'Hap' or 'A Plaint to Man' devoid of emotion –

> And why unblooms the best hope ever sown?

51

We are talking about their relative qualities. A coinage such as 'unblooms' may work or not: personally I like it. But whatever your verdict, such a word will draw attention to itself because it is unnatural: more simply and appropriately because it has been *thought up*. Such a word will always indicate the presence of intellectual effort. It tells us that the thought has not found an easy, natural expression. In order to express himself, Hardy has had to fight with the language. And rightly or wrongly, most of us believe that such fighting is proper to philosophizing, though not to the expression of love. It is this quality of visible, effortful thought in the diction which makes the problem of tone as identified by Pritchard easier to tackle in this present kind of poetry. The deliberation that went to such words' coining must be reflected in the way we say them. It is easy enough to say 'unblooms' in this context with an emphasis that makes the unwelcome negative very pungent. But in a context where sardonic emphasis is not appropriate, the problem is much trickier.

3.14 This is the final section of your work on Hardy, and some kind of summing up would seem appropriate. Yet few poets discourage such a thing more, partly because his material is so diverse, but more importantly because some of his late, philosophical poems virtually forbid it, by discountenancing all idea of an ending. Read 'The Absolute Explains' (p 166) and 'So, Time' (p 169), about which Creighton says:

> . . . he finds in relativity a provisionally optimistic solution to the problem of time and death that so oppressed him earlier. 'Relativity – that things and events always were, are, and will be (e.g. Emma, Mother and Father are living still in the past)'.[4] (Creighton p 344.)

Hardy's notion of relativity is of course very much simplified:

> And now comes Einstein with a notion –
>   Not yet quite clear
>   To many here –
> That there's no time, no space, no motion,
>   Nor rathe nor late,
>   Nor square nor straight,
> But just a sort of bending-ocean.
> ('Drinking Song', Creighton p 178.)

Neither 'The Absolute Explains', nor 'So, Time' is a particularly successful poem, though you can usefully test in reading them the value of what I had to say about the appropriateness of Hardy's deliberative style to his more overtly philosophical poetry. As you might expect, the longer poem comes to life when it revitalizes the past:

> There were those songs, a score times sung,
>   With all their tripping tunes,
> There were the laughters once that rung
>   There those unmatched full moons,
>   Those idle noons!

But Hardy had no need of any theory of relativity to revive the past, because in a sense he had mastered it long before he heard of Einstein. The theory of relativity was later to fascinate T. S. Eliot; it is a pivotal theme in some of his most important

[4]From Hardy *Life*, p 419.

religious and philosophic verse. But it appealed to Hardy because it coincided with his emotional experience, which included a distinctly *personal* notion of relativity. Read again 'At Castle Boterel' (p 62) paying particular attention to how Hardy handles that slipperiest of all concepts, time.

3.15 Particularly dexterous is the use of tenses to ease the distinction between then and now. The first sentence describing what he recalls (i.e. what is in the past) is still in the present tense: 'We climb the road/Behind a chaise'. In the third stanza, the notion of future is very fluid. It is both the past's future (what that moment led to); and the present's future – for the significance of that moment will outlive the present day of drizzle and last 'till hope is dead,/And feeling fled'.

You may have already read Donald Davie's difficult but important commentary on the phrase 'A time of such quality' (given in Appendix 2). The phrase implies the survival of *all* the hill's moments, recalled perhaps by the 'thousands more' who have climbed it. But 'one mind' (Hardy's) is convinced that if all the hill's moments are imagined strung in sequence like beads on a string, then one in particular is pre-eminent. With no false modesty, and only a punctuation mark to draw attention to the sheer nerve of his claim, he asserts

> But what they record in colour and cast
>   Is – that we two passed.

More: he increases the time-scale to the pre-human, the geological, the unimaginable:

> Primaeval rocks form the road's steep border,
>   And much have they faced there, first and last,
> Of the transitory in Earth's long order . . .

Yet still he insists that to his mind, the rocks mean only that 'we two passed'. It is very difficult to paraphrase the claims of this poem. He is *not* simply saying that the rocks remind him of a happier past. The phantom figure possesses the greater reality. Yet it is not also true to say that just as the original moment (which retains its reality) *passed*, so too the moment when this past reality is recognized is itself transitory, and is passing as the poem ends:

> I look and see it there, shrinking, shrinking,
>   I look back at it amid the rain
> For the very last time . . .

3.16 It is in 'At Castle Boterel' that the idea of time is most insistently expressed. But in all the poems of 1912–13, and indeed in many more, the survival of the past simultaneously with the present is the theme which brings Hardy's poetry to its most moving pitch. It is not enough to say that he was moved by memory. We have to notice that it is always the past in specific relation to some later time. Usually the later time is more bitter, and drabber than the earlier, so that the past frequently seems more real than the present. And when we think of Hardy's ghosts, we must remember that Emma survived as many ghosts – as the girl he first knew, and the woman as he last saw her: and that, too, simultaneously. But it is the contrast, the insistence on a significant simultaneity of past and present that I want to stress. Many other poets, notably Wordsworth, have found in memory the sources of their power. But none has laid so much emphasis on the relation between past and present.

3.17 A short, late, jaunty poem, 'Our Old Friend Dualism', is worth reading at this point, because it gives a very explicit clue to a feature implicit in the majority of Hardy's poems. All the explanation it needs is in Creighton's notes. Of course I am not suggesting that anything as slight as 'Our Old Friend Dualism' is, as it were, the linchpin of the *Collected Works*. But it helps to draw attention to a consistent kind of dualism that might otherwise be difficult to spot. I said that Hardy is acutely conscious of sequence. But this can be expanded: Hardy is acutely conscious of contrasting or comparing states of all kinds. Big things are compared with small (and vice versa); things as they are with things as they were, or might be or might have been; the individual is seen in relation to the universal; the chance or accident is held up against the infinite number of things that did not happen. Hardy habitually sets one thing off against another. Indeed, what he seizes in an event is so often precisely that quality which can make one half of a contrast. For example, what do you think made Hardy want to write the following poem:

The Gap in the White (178–)

Something had cracked in her mouth as she slept,
Having danced with the Prince long, and sipped his gold tass;
And she woke in alarm, and quick, breathlessly, leapt
    Out of bed to the glass.

And there, in the blue dawn, her mouth now displayed
    To her woe, in the white
Level line of her teeth, a black gap she had made
    In dream's nervous bite.

'O how can I meet him to-morrow!' she said.
'I'd won him – yes, yes! Now, alas, he is lost!'
(That age knew no remedy.) Duly her dread
    Proved the truth, to her cost.

And if you could go and examine her grave
    You'd find the gap there,
But not understand, now that science can save,
    Her unbounded despair.

3.18 You may well have found it difficult to take seriously. I admit that I have been glad to fall back on the complaint Hardy several times made, that far too many poems that were intended as jokes were taken seriously. And yet it has got to be taken seriously, or not at all, as the last stanza makes clear: if you do not understand 'Her unbounded despair', then there is a failure of sympathy in you. Of course, you may not be able to take it. Perhaps, after all, its outstanding characteristic is its foolishness, something the critic of poetry is seldom called on to make up his mind about. Here are two more opinions: C. D. Lewis (*The Lyrical Poetry of Thomas Hardy* pp 155–74) says 'The Gap in the White' helps us to understand Hardy's 'unbounded sympathy' even if 'gossip lures [him] on to the most intractable subjects' for poetry. Edward Shanks ('Songs of Joy') asks who else 'could have seen the tragedy implicit in this collocation of love and dentistry? . . . Who else, having chosen it, would have dared the ruthless prose of that parenthesis? The answer is: only another man who loved the details of life even to greediness as Hardy did.'[5]

3.19 I am quite sure these observations are just, but I am also convinced that what made the anecdote especially attractive to Hardy was the fact that it bristles with all sorts of possibilities of *contrast*: between love and rejection; glamour and obscurity; beauty and its loss; above all, with things as they were, and things as they are,

[5]Both quotations are cited in J. O. Bailey *The Poetry of Thomas Hardy*.

'now that science can save'. I have a hunch (and that, of course, is all it can be) that the inception of this poem was with something that drew Hardy's attention to the marvels of modern dentistry. (He was, after all, always fascinated by technological advance.) There is a little evidence for this in a letter of 1899: 'You will remember my saying I had never had any necessity for a dentist? As a judgement, about a fortnight ago a front tooth came out – absolutely without a flaw in it. I have done nothing to remedy it, and do not intend to.' (Again, Bailey is the source for this quotation.) Hardy, of course, had not sipped anyone's gold tass.

3.20   Perhaps we have spent over-long on a poem that Creighton has omitted for reasons that need no guessing. But go back for a moment to two poems looked at in Part 1 Section 4: 'A Sheep Fair' (p 7) and 'Ice on the Highway' (p 13). The *Postscript* of the first still seems redundant, but might it not have been an impulse for contrast that made Hardy add it? And in 'Ice on the Highway' might it not be that Hardy placed more emphasis on the last line than the reader who takes it as a piece of simple description is bound to do?

> Yet loud their laughter as they stagger and slide!

3.21   In some poems the antithetical tendency is more prominent. In 'A Wife in London' contrast forms the centre of the poem – is indeed its very subject.

I

She sits in the tawny vapour
    That the Thames-side lanes have uprolled,
    Behind whose webby fold on fold
Like a waning taper
    The street lamp glimmers cold.

A messenger's knock cracks smartly,
    Flashed news is in her hand
    Of meaning it dazes to understand
Though shaped so shortly:
    He – has fallen – in the far South Land . . .

II

'Tis the morrow; the fog hangs thicker,
    The postman nears and goes:
    A letter is brought whose lines disclose
By the firelight flicker
    His hand, whom the worm now knows.

Fresh – firm – penned in highest feather –
    Page-full of his hoped return,
    And of home-planned jaunts by brake and burn
In the summer weather,
    And of new love that they would learn.

It is a slight thing, but surely it is beautifully done. That news of death should travel faster than news from the living is just the kind of irony that would appeal to Hardy. Yet that is far from being the only contrast: the irony is softened and enriched by the patterns of contrasting light that run throughout the poem. The 'waning taper', the coldly glimmering lamp both strike a note of foreboding. 'Flashed news' is a strange periphrasis for a telegram, but surely justified because it signifies so much more than the normal word could. 'Flashed' even brings the telegram into a kind of relation with the different sorts of light in the poem. 'South-land' again seems at first unnecessary, unless it be for the rhyme. But the suggestions of warmth in the word South make an important contrast with the wintry coldness of London – and in the second part, with the summer which the now-dead soldier had hoped for.

In Part II the thicker fog suggests her new isolation, deeper than that of mere separation. The contents of the letter are revealed 'By the firelight flicker' – the protective domestic warmth needed to keep the winter away, so different from the flash, almost suggesting a kind of strange lightning which brought news of death. Everywhere there is contrast: the news of death is 'flashed' – quickly; the letter is brought by the postman who 'nears and goes' – a much slower movement. The telegram is put into her hand; the letter comes from 'His hand, whom the worm now knows'. Finally, the greatest contrast is not articulated at all; it is between her sorrowing, which is nowhere explicitly referred to, and the 'new love that they would learn'.

3.22   Look now at the exquisite 'Logs on the Hearth – A Memory of a Sister', and examine how it gains in richness by the contrasts it contains.

Even if you do not agree with my thesis, I hope you liked the poem. Turn now to 'Neutral Tones', a very early poem, which describes powerfully and even frighteningly, a single, intense moment – though what the intensity is about, we hardly know.

3.23   In the extract from his book on Hardy in the Course Reader, Douglas Brown makes some finely perceptive comments about Hardy's ability to seize a particular moment, and the peculiar power he derives from the apparently simple act of setting it down. I want to add the suggestion that what makes these moments so powerful, so much bigger than they seem, is that they are packed with contrasts. The single moment and the simple perception, are *stretched*. Almost literally it is tension that makes some of Hardy's captured moments so nearly unbearable. The moment remains, fixed and defined, but it can be enlarged sometimes almost to infinity, by the distances between the contrasts it contains. I have emphasized the deliberation in Hardy's style; I want now to stress the degree of consciousness that manipulates these ever-recurring contrasts. In 'Neutral Tones' they are kept on a very tight rein; as the title indicates, the spectrum is not wide enough to allow great variety. And so the poem is, in a way, *about* emotion under some sort of restraint, and a kind of dullness that has fallen on passion: the limit of the contrast is not white and *black*, but white and grey. The tension is at its most acute in stanza three, where the two middle lines approach the condition of oxymoron (which the Concise Oxford Dictionary defines as 'Figure of speech with pointed conjunction of seeming contradictories.')

> Alive enough to have strength to die;
> And a grin of bitterness swept thereby . . .

The poem is very oddly shaped, for its last two lines apparently repeat, in a condensed form, the substance of the previous part of the poem. The sense of the first line and a half of the final stanza is a little ambiguous. It means, I think, that any *subsequent* 'keen lessons that love deceives' remind him of the first lesson. So the major antithesis is not so much a contrast, as the placing of an incident against itself. The instinct for a dualistic pattern is still strong.

3.24   However, we must be wary of the word dualism, for it suggests a definite philosophy, whereas we know that Hardy had none. The variety of attitudes in his religious and philosophical poetry suggests a man constantly looking for an answer, and finding only another paradox. Yet we have to conclude that paradox suited Hardy, and that he found a deep pleasure to the imagination in the contemplation of the way in which life deploys incongruities, and confronts opposites with each other. Look, for example (the final example) at one of the strangest, and yet most moving of all Hardy's poems: 'To an Unborn Pauper Child'.

The unborn child seems like another kind of ghost. Once again, the diction claims our attention. There is the marvellous, startling opening, which Hardy so often achieves:

> Breathe not, hid Heart: cease silently

There are the oddities (Time-wraiths, theeward) and the awkward inversions (Explain none can). Above all, there is *range*: from a kind of formal quaintness:

> The Doomsters heap
> Travails and teens around us here,
> And Time-wraiths turn our songsingings to fear.

– to a splendid, stark fortissimo:

> Thou wilt thy ignorant entry make
> Though skies spout fire and blood and nations quake.

– to a quiet, tender simplicity, quite free of all bitterness:

> But I am weak as thou and bare;
> No man can change the common lot to rare.

Without this flexibility, would the amazing turn at the end be as convincing? For the language itself proclaims the inconsistencies and incongruities of existence. I suggested that the unborn pauper child is another kind of ghost; surely, here, as in the love poems (not *only* those to his dead wife) Hardy is at his best when he confronts not just the immediate realities of life, but those other realities which belong to the irrational, or the superrational; when, in spite of what seems to be the evidence, he can see alongside the harshness of life, the kind of alternative which ends 'To an Unborn Pauper Child'?

> . . . And such are we –
> Unreasoning, sanguine, visionary –
>   That I can hope
>   Health, love, friends, scope
> In full for thee; can dream thou'lt find
> Joys seldom yet attained by humankind!

Here probability has been held up to a scale of sublime possibilities. Hardy's view of life was not simple at all; but neither had he worked out a systematic philosophy. As I said before, he saw pattern, but no meaning. This is something you will of course need to test for yourself. I suggest you spend half an hour or so either re-reading poems you have particularly admired, or picking others at random. How often is this instinct for alternatives, opposites, contrasts, *really* present? Does it suggest to you a muddled vision, or a courageous act of the will, which is not daunted by inexplicable contrarieties? And finally, are you satisfied by a poet who implies that all he can do is record his experience that for every positive there is a negative; for everything that happens an infinity of possibilities? To be truly great, must a poet make up his mind and stick to it?

APPENDIX 1   A BRIEF NOTE ON BALLADS

So many critics make some reference to the relationship between Hardy's poetry and the ballad tradition that a brief reminder of the nature of that tradition may be useful. The best way of improving your knowledge of ballads, of course, is to read them, and the two most generally accessible collections are the new *Oxford Book of Ballads*, ed. James Kinsley; and the Penguin *Border Ballads*, ed. William Beattie. (The finest ballads in English come from Southern Scotland.)

A ballad tells a story, which may have a basis in fairy-lore, in legend, or in historical fact. Maybe some that have become legendary once had a strong basis in fact, for the origins of many are obscure. The authors, or originators, of traditional ballads are not known by name, and usually the date of the original composition can only be guessed at if the events described are historical. Most ballads as we know them are probably not as they were originally composed, for they have been handed down orally, and successive generations may have altered or added to them. We usually know them in a printed form, the work of the great antiquarian collectors who felt that orally preserved traditions were in danger of extinction. The work is still going on, and 'new' traditional ballads are still being discovered and recorded.

There is another kind of ballad, *the broadside*, related to the traditional kind, but with the essential difference that it cannot exist without print – the very thing that has either saved or arrested the traditional ballad, depending on your point of view. The word broadside refers to the form in which they were distributed: a sheet printed on one side only. Broadsides were common from the late sixteenth century to the middle of the nineteenth. They imitated the ballad form for political and topical purposes, and were in effect, a form of popular journalism.

The most common ballad form is easily described. The standard verse form is a quatrain, often with only one rhyming pair (abcb) and roughly iambic lines of eight and six syllables alternately. But it is really the style and tone which are more important, and more difficult to describe. Ballads treat their subjects dramatically. It is a rather ruthless technique, which preserves the important points, and leaves out what connects them – though occasionally an apparently inconsequential detail may survive. It is easy to understand how oral transmission may have eroded the connecting passages, and left only the high, memorable points of the narrative. Hence the frequent sense of mystery attaching to ballads: we are not told how the story moves from one event to another – they simply happen.

The traditional ballads are stirring, but unemotional and impersonal. If they are the work of generations, then of course they cannot represent an individual's personality, though they may express something which has belonged to a cultural group over a long period of time. Topical broadsides, on the other hand, are frequently sentimental, and political ones usually have a propaganda purpose. But even these are seldom in any way personal. Sentiment will sell the 'Farewell to the World of Richard Bishop' (written about 1860, and quoted in *The Common Muse*, ed. V. de Sola Pinto and A. E. Rodway, Penguin, 1965):

> Farewell, vain world, I now must leave you,
>   Farewell, my friends and neighbours all,
> Around Forest Hill no more you'll see me,
>   The hangman's voice on me does call;
> Saying, Richard Bishop, now be ready,
>   To die upon the fatal tree,
> Oh, aged only one and twenty,
>   What a dreadful sight to see.

Propaganda sells a cause, and it was in the area of politics that the broadside ballad began to turn into the 'literary ballad', because so many of the most important poets of the eighteenth and nineteenth centuries with some public cause to plead used the familiar traditional forms to reach an audience that might have been intimidated by a 'higher' style.

APPENDIX 2   A SELECTION OF VIEWS ON SOME OF THE POEMS OF 1912–13

The following quotations have been put together as an alternative guide to the poems of 1912–13: *Veteris vestigia flammae.*

'AFTER A JOURNEY'

1 . . . it is not declamatory. The point should in justice lead on to a positive formulation, and this may not come as readily; certain stylistic characteristics that may at first strike the reader as oddities and clumsinesses tend to delay the recognition of the convincing intimate naturalness. It turns out, however, that the essential ethos of the manner is given in

Where you will next be there is no knowing . . . ,

This intimacy we are at first inclined to describe as 'conversational', only to replace that adjective by 'self-communing' when we have recognized that, even when Hardy (and it is significant that we say 'Hardy') addresses the 'ghost' he is still addressing himself. And it shouldn't take long to recognize that the marked idiosyncrasy of idiom and diction going with the intimacy of tone achieves some striking precisions and felicities. Consider, for instance, the verb in

Facing round about me everywhere . . .

There is nothing that strikes us as odd in that 'facing', but it is a use created for the occasion, and when we look into its unobtrusive naturalness it turns out to have a positive and 'inevitable' rightness, the analysis of which involves a precise account of the 'ghost's' status – which in its turn involves a precise account of the highly specific situation defined by the poem.

Then again, there is that noun in the fourth line which (I can testify) has offended readers not incapable of recognizing its felicity:

And the unseen waters' ejaculations awe me.

'Ejaculations' gives with vivid precision the sound that 'awes' Hardy; the slap of the waves on the rocky walls; the slap with its prolonging reverberant syllables – the hollow voice, in fact, that, in stanza three, 'seems to call out to me from forty years ago' (and the hollowness rings significantly through the poem).

In fact, the difference first presenting itself as an absence of declamatory manner and tone, examined, leads to the perception of positive characteristics – precisions of concrete realization, specificities, complexities – that justify the judgment I now advance; Hardy's poem. . . . is seen to have a great advantage in *reality.*

(F. R. Leavis (1952) 'Reality and Sincerity, Notes in the Analysis of Poetry', *Scrutiny,* Vol 19.)

2　The self-communing tone is established in the first four lines, and there is no change when Hardy passes from the 'its' of the second line to the 'you' of the fifth. He remains 'lonely, lost' throughout the poem: that is not a state which is altered by his communion (if that is the word) with the 'ghost'. The loneliness and the desolation are far from being mitigated by the 'viewing' in memory; for the condition of the 'viewing' is Hardy's full realizing contemplation of the woman's irremediable absence – of the fact that she is dead.

(F. R. Leavis (1952) 'Reality and Sincerity, Notes in the Analysis of Poetry', *Scrutiny*, Vol 19.)

3　Leavis takes pains to demonstrate that what looks like awkwardness is really felicity, that 'the unseen waters' ejaculations awe me' gives with 'vivid precision' the slap of the waves on the rocky walls. Yet the line seems a mouthful, a bit of quaintness still clings to 'ejaculations', especially with the 'awe me/draw me' rhyme so unashamed of itself. I don't think, that is, we should decide that the style simply *looks* awkward, but is *really* profoundly natural, delicately right – or whatever terms a critic uses to tell us we weren't looking and listening hard enough. At least in my experience the stanzas after many readings still feel odd and strange, and remarkably so . . .

One of the things Time might deride is the act of making up poetic messages to pass on to a voiceless ghost in the hopes that it will pass them back to you; and 'all's closed now' moves towards a condition of voicelessness which knows no words are adequate. But the poem keeps on talking as Hardy follows the ghost. . . .

Can we call this distinguished poetry while admitting that it contains some grotesque effects which we can only accept by saying, as it were, 'Oh that's the way Hardy sometimes writes – he's that sort of poet'? It is hard to read without grimacing – and at such a crucial moment in the poem – the beginning of the final adjuration: 'Trust me, I mind not, though Life lours/The bringing me here' – and then to have 'lours' triumphantly rhymed with 'flowers'! Everything is not perfectly executed in this fine and moving poem, yet the rough spots matter little more than they do in Wordsworth's Immortality Ode. 'After a Journey' is astonishing for the way it lives with the language of music hall popular lyric – 'When you were all aglow' – and manages to bring it alive, generously definitive.

(William H. Pritchard (1972) 'Hardy's anonymous sincerity', *Agenda* Vol 10 nos 2 and 3. An extract from the same article quoted at greater length in the Course Reader.)

4　The identification of human life and loving with the natural and the seasonal reaches its climax in 'After a Journey'. The decline of a human relationship is presented as an inevitable seasonal deterioration, the harshness of Autumn following upon the 'sweets' of Summer, with its 'fair hour', 'fair weather' and 'paths through flowers'. Unusually for these poems of haunting the woman's facial colouring is here noted but it is described in terms of natural vegetation – 'nut-coloured hair' and 'rose-flush'. The 'thin ghost' of this poem is the least ambiguous of all Hardy's phantom presences. No doubt is cast upon her actuality as in the other poems of haunting which explains why Hardy forsakes his usual silhouette presentation and focuses instead on the woman's countenance 'facing round about him everywhere'. The phantom woman, however, retains her habitual elusiveness, being depicted as a will o' the wisp luring the speaker on at its 'whim', 'up the cliff, down', the 'ignis fatuus' being in this case a 'rose-flush coming and going'. The will o' the wisp metaphor perfectly captures the combination of the wraith-like and impalpable with the spatially elusive and Hardy's subtle mastery of diction is evident in the economy of the phrase, 'rose-flush coming and going', which refers simultaneously to the irregular flicker of the phosphorescent light, the pulsations of the woman's response to her lover and her continual 'flitting movements': 'Where you will be next there's no knowing'. As in some of the other poems of haunting already discussed, the natural background is evoked in such a way as to create a metaphorical context which sustains the phantom theme. The presence of a 'voiceless ghost', seen but unheard at first, is rendered more credible by the ready acceptance of the 'unseen waters' ejaculations' which though audible are invisible. The word 'ejaculations' combines the sense of jetting movement and brief emotional utterance. 'The waterfall above which the mist-bow shone' also conjures up an impression of an evanescent presence hovering above the cascade similar to the ghostly form now 'flitting here to see'. The act of communing with the dead, too, seems less extraordinary in the context of a cave 'with a voice still so hollow/That it seems to call out . . . from forty years ago'.

(Maire A. Quinn (1974) 'The Personal Past in the Poetry of Thomas Hardy and Edward Thomas' *Critical Quarterly*, Summer 1974.)

'THE VOICE'

1   *The Voice* . . . seems to start dangerously with a crude popular lilt, but this is turned into a subtle movement by the prosaic manner of the content, a manner that elsewhere would have been Hardy's characteristic gaucherie. . . .

By the end of [the] second stanza the bare matter-of-fact testament has already subdued the rhythm; the shift of stress on the rime ('view you then', 'knew you then') has banished the jingle from it. In the next stanza we have an instance of his odd word-coinages . . . 'existlessness' (which he afterwards, and, I think, unfortunately, changed to 'wan wistlessness') is a questionable word, a characteristic eccentricity of invention; and yet here it sounds right. The touch that there may still be about the poem of what would normally have been rustic stiffness serves as a kind of guarantee of integrity. And then there is the exquisite modulation into the last stanza.

Hardy needed a strong, immediately personal impulse before he could transform his innocent awkwardness in this way.

(F. R. Leavis (1972) *New Bearings in English Poetry*, Penguin. Set book.)

2   We have here, as we usually have in Hardy, a poem composed in antinomial terms: present is set against past, life against death, hope against despair. The poem is unusual, however, in that the distinction between the terms is most striking in its metrical aspect. Hardy was usually content to continue in the stanza form in which he began, but here he uses a change of form for significant effect. The first three stanzas are set in the triple rhythm which Hardy used frequently, but not often very well. The rhythm is at first fairly mellifluous – the first stanza scans easily without any serious problems – but becomes rougher in the third stanza, with extra syllables and juxtaposed stresses. The final stanza, the 'Present' term of the poem, is set in an altogether different meter, which 'falters forward' irregularly, as the speaker does . . . .

But to a reader familiar with metrical experimentation of the last fifty years, Hardy's venture into organic form must seem rather a timid one, which did not stray very far from metrical traditionalism.

(Samuel Hynes (1961) *The Pattern of Hardy's Poetry*, Chapel Hill, University of North Carolina Press, p 78.)

3   Natural imagery is invoked in a more ambiguous manner in one of the finest of all Hardy's poems on the theme of haunting, 'The Voice'. Here the possibility of seeing the dead woman and hearing her call is rendered plausible by her approximation

to what is undefined and evanescent in the natural scene in life. The 'original air-blue gown' which she wore when meeting her lover endowed her with an aura of insubstantiality during her lifetime and also assimilated her to the elemental 'air'. Living, she thus appeared incorporeal a phantom liable at any moment to dissolve 'into existlessness'. After her death a haze of blue air in a place associated with her will seem her presence rendered visible. The 'double entendre' of the poem's opening apostrophe, 'Woman much missed', also assimilates the dead woman to what is most ethereal and elusive in the natural scene, fusing in one telling phrase those suggestions of absence and vaguely apprehended presence which are central to the poem's haunting theme. The dead woman's voice, like her gown, may also be composed only of air, may be 'only the breeze in its listlessness'. Just as the woman is evoked in terms of the elemental and the natural so the breeze with its 'listlessness' partakes of the attributes of the human world, and the happy relationship of the lovers, too, may be described in the atmospheric terms: 'When our day was fair'. This interchangeability of human and natural characteristics which forms the basis of so many of Hardy's poems of haunting here concludes in the almost total inter-penetration of man and nature. The lover groping towards the ghost of the dead woman enters into the realm of natural death and decay ('leaves around me falling'). The verbal echo of 'faltering' in 'falling' enacts the fusion of the human and the natural, while the 'thin' oozing of the wind in the next line recalls the gossamer appearance of both lady and ghost. Finally the questing man, the elusive spectre and the decaying Autumnal landscape are inextricably blended in the assonantal echoes of the last stanza: the man *faltering forward*, the wind blowing through the *thorn* from *norward*, leaves *falling* and the woman *calling*.

(Maire A. Quinn (1974) 'The Personal Past in the Poetry of Thomas Hardy and Edward Thomas', *Critical Quarterly*, Summer 1974.)

'AT CASTLE BOTEREL'

1   It is from the perspective of 'Where the Picnic Was' that J. Hillis Miller is able to detect 'the poet's gradual recognition, recorded explicitly in "At Castle Boterel" and "The Phantom Horsewoman", that Emma exists not as an objective ghost which any man might see, but in the poet's mind. Though the "primaeval rocks" by a certain roadside record in their colour and shape the fact that he and his lady passed there one March night long ago, this imprint of the transitory on the permanent is visible only "to one mind", the mind of the poet in whose vision "one phantom figure/Remains on the slope", though time, "in mindless rote", has long since obliterated the reality'.[1] . . . I repudiate such a reading totally, and with a sort of fury. What is more to the point is that the poem itself repudiates the parody thus foisted upon it. . . .

The crucial word is 'quality' – 'a time of such *quality*'. For the qualitative has no existence outside of a mind that registers it. And quality is therefore invulnerable to time, since the 'rote' by which Time works is mindless. (All that time can destroy is 'substance' – a philosophical word to set against the other philosophical word, 'quality'.) Miller with bland audacity writes a minus for every plus in the poem, and a plus for every minus. When he speaks of 'this imprint of the transitory on the permanent' he takes as self-evidently transitory what the poem declares to be permanent – that is, quality: and he takes as permanent what the poem thinks of as comparatively transient – that is to say, the primaeval rocks, long-lasting though they are. 'Well, but' (I hear the protests) 'what happens to the quality

---

[1] J. Hillis Miller (1970) *Thomas Hardy, Distance and Desire*, Harvard University Press, p 251.

when the one mind has gone, in which alone it had existence? What happens to it when Hardy is dead?' Who shall say? It's at this point that everything hinges on whether the reality that Hardy explores is psychological merely, or metaphysical. If Hardy is concerned only with psychological reality, as Miller and most other readers assume, then he is saying only that he will remember Emma, and the quality of this moment he shared with her, until the day he dies. Which is touching: but hardly worth saying at such length. But if the 'time of such quality' persists indestructible in a metaphysical reality, then it is *truly* indestructible – because a man's mind survives the death of his body, or because quality exists as perceived by a Divine Mind, or . . . The poet does not have to decide these matters; he does not have to decide the mode in which the quality will persist after his death, it is enough for him to affirm his conviction that persist it will.

(Donald Davie (1972) 'Hardy's Virgilian Purples', *Agenda*, Vol 10 nos 2 and 3 p 154.)

2   . . . his method in 'At Castle Boterel' . . . makes use of a . . . combination of circumstances to conjure up a spectral presence. Here, too, the living woman is depicted only in outline, 'a girlish form', so that the transition to her 'phantom-figure' is easily achieved. 'At Castle Boterel' also employs similar atmospheric effects of misty rainfall. It is noteworthy that the original love-scene which the speaker recalls took place 'in dry March weather' but its re-enactment is possible only in a 'drizzle' which casts a filmy haze over present day actualities so that the realities of temporal change do not obtrude themselves on the vision of the past and the possible emptiness of the road is blurred from sight. The word 'fading' in the phrase 'I look behind at the fading byway' suggests both increasing distance and waning light.

(Maire A. Quinn (1974) 'The Personal Past in the Poetry of Thomas Hardy and Edward Thomas', *Critical Quarterly*, Summer 1974.)

'THE GOING'

1   The 'Going' of the title is picked up by 'be gone' in the first stanza; this is linked with 'your great going' in the next; and all these variations on 'go' and 'going' and 'gone' are consummated six lines from the end in the utterly characteristic, audacious, and harrowing line: 'Unchangeable. It must go.' It asks a poet, not just a great and daring technician, to ring such changes on so common a word, and by his changes to graph the progress of a pain from the first to last through his poem. And yet if this is the nerve of the poem, the hidden form of its unfolding, that form is (I think) not merely hidden and decently cloaked, but positively *impeded* by the overt form with its intricate symmetries. Accordingly, though with the greatest hesitation, I find the imperious verbal engineer still, even here, thwarting the true and truly suffering poet.

(Donald Davie (1973) *Thomas Hardy and British Poetry*, Routledge & Kegan Paul.)

REFERENCES AND FURTHER READING

Bailey, J. O. (1970) *The Poetry of Thomas Hardy*, Chapel Hill, University of North Carolina Press.

Brown, Douglas (1954) *Thomas Hardy*, Longmans, Green & Co. (The book from which the Course Reader extract is taken.)

Creighton, T. R. M. (ed.) (1974) *Poems of Thomas Hardy, A New Selection*, Macmillan (set book).

Davie, Donald (1972) *Thomas Hardy and British Poetry*, Oxford University Press.

Hardy, Florence Emily (1962) *The Life of Thomas Hardy*, Macmillan.

Hynes, Samuel (1961) *The Pattern of Hardy's Poetry*, Chapel Hill, University of North Carolina Press.

Larkin, P. (1966) 'Wanted: Good Hardy Critic', *Critical Quarterly* Vol 8 no. 2, Summer 1966.

Leavis, F. R. (1952) 'Reality and Sincerity, Notes in the Analysis of Poetry', *Scrutiny* Vol 19, 1952.

Leavis, F. R. (1972) *New Bearings in English Poetry*, Penguin (set book).

Lewis, C. Day (1951) *The Lyrical Poetry of Thomas Hardy*, Proceedings of the British Academy XXXVII pp 155–74.

Martin, Graham and Furbank, P. N. (eds.) (1975) *Twentieth Century Poetry: Critical Essays and Documents*, The Open University Press (Course Reader).

Pound, Ezra (1961) *The ABC of Reading*, Faber.

Press, John (1969) *A Map of Modern English Verse*, Oxford University Press (set book).

Pritchard, W. H. (1972) 'Hardy's anonymous sincerity' *Agenda* Vol 10 nos 2 and 3. (Reprinted in the Course Reader.)

Quinn, Maire A. (1974) 'The Personal Past in the Poetry of Thomas Hardy and Edward Thomas' *Critical Quarterly* Vol 16 no. 2, Summer 1974.

Ransom, John Crowe (1940) 'Honey and Gall' *The Southern Review* VI.

Shanks, Edward (1928) 'Songs of Joy' *Saturday Review* CXLVI November 1928.

Stead, C. K. (1964) *The New Poetic*, Hutchinson (set book).

Taylor, A. J. P. (1965) *English History 1919–45*, Oxford University Press.

A larger, useful bibliography is included in Creighton, pp 353–4.

ACKNOWLEDGEMENTS

Grateful acknowledgement is made to the following sources for material used in these units:

Agenda Editions for extract from Donald Davie, 'Hardy's Virgilian purples' and William H. Pritchard, 'Hardy's anonymous sincerity', *Agenda*, Spring-Summer, 1972; Faber and Faber and Farrar, Straus & Giroux Inc. for Philip Larkin, 'Sad steps' in *High Windows*, Faber; Faber and Faber and Harcourt Brace Jovanovich for extracts from T. S. Eliot, 'Tradition and the individual talent' in *Selected Essays*, new edition, copyright 1932, 1936, 1950 by Harcourt Brace Jovanovich Inc., copyright 1960, 1964 by T. S. Eliot. Reprinted by permission of the publishers; Faber and Faber and Random House Inc. for W. H. Auden, 'Their lonely betters' in *Collected Shorter Poems 1927–1957*, Faber; extracts from F. E. Hardy, *The Life of Thomas Hardy*, and Hardy's poems and excerpts from poems quoted from *Collected Poems of Thomas Hardy*, reprinted by permission of the Hardy Estate, Macmillan, London and Basingstoke, The Macmillan Company of Canada, and Macmillan Publishing Co. Inc, New York; New Directions Publishing Corp, New York for Wilfred Owen, 'Strange meeting' in *Collected Poems*, copyright 1946, 1963 Chatto and Windus; the author for extract from Maire A. Quinn, 'The personal past in the poetry of Thomas Hardy and Edward Thomas', *Critical Quarterly*, Summer 1974.